WeightWatchers®

Fresh and fabulous recipes for every day

Soups & Salads

First published in Great Britain by Simon & Schuster UK Ltd, 2012
A CBS Company

www.simonandschuster.co.uk

Simon & Schuster Australia, Sydney
Simon & Schuster India, New Delhi

Weight Watchers Publications: Cheryl Jackson, Jane Griffiths, Martha Hughes, Selena Makepeace, Nina McKerlie and Imogen Prescott.

Recipes written by: Recipes written by: Sue Ashworth, Sue Beveridge, Tamsin Burnett-Hall, Cas Clarke, Siân Davies, Roz Denny, Nicola Graimes, Becky Johnson, Kim Morphew, Joy Skipper, Penny Stephens and Wendy Veale as well as Weight Watchers Leaders and Members..

Photography by: Iain Bagwell, Steve Baxter, Steve Lee, Juliet Piddington and William Shaw.
Project editor: Nicki Lampon.
Design and typesetting: Geoff Fennell.

Colour reproduction by Dot Gradations Ltd, UK.
Printed and bound in China.

A CIP catalogue for this book is available from the British Library

ISBN 978-0-85720-933-7

1 2 3 4 5 6 7 8 9 10

Pictured on the title page: Warm goat's cheese salad p140.
Pictured on the Introduction: Manhattan seafood soup p54,
Chicken and vegetable chowder p52, Chilli, crab and mango salad p94.

WeightWatchers®

Fresh and fabulous recipes for every day

Soups & Salads

SIMON &
SCHUSTER
ILLUSTRATED

London · New York · Sydney · Toronto · New Delhi

A CBS COMPANY

Weight Watchers **ProPoints** Weight Loss System is a simple way to lose weight. As part of the Weight Watchers **ProPoints** plan you'll enjoy eating delicious, healthy, filling foods that help to keep you feeling satisfied for longer and in control of your portions.

Ⓥ This symbol denotes a vegetarian recipe and assumes that, where relevant, free range eggs, vegetarian cheese, vegetarian virtually fat free fromage frais, vegetarian low fat crème fraîche and vegetarian low fat yogurts are used. Virtually fat free fromage frais, low fat crème fraîche and low fat yogurts may contain traces of gelatine so they are not always vegetarian. Please check the labels.

❄ This symbol denotes a dish that can be frozen. Unless otherwise stated, you can freeze the finished dish for up to 3 months. Defrost thoroughly and reheat until the dish is piping hot throughout.

Recipe notes

Egg size: Medium, unless otherwise stated.

Raw eggs: Only the freshest eggs should be used. Pregnant women, the elderly and children should avoid recipes with eggs that are not fully cooked or raw.

All fruits and vegetables: Medium, unless otherwise stated.

Stock: Stock cubes are used in recipes, unless otherwise stated. These should be prepared according to packet instructions.

Recipe timings: These are approximate and meant to be guidelines. Please note that the preparation time includes all the steps up to and following the main cooking time(s).

Microwaves: Timings and temperatures are for a standard 800 W microwave. If necessary, adjust your own microwave.

Low fat spread: Where a recipe states to use a low fat spread, a light spread with a fat content of no less than 38% should be used.

Low fat soft cheese: Where low fat soft cheese is specified in a recipe, this refers to soft cheese with a fat content of less than 5%.

Contents

Introduction   6

Light and colourful soups   12

Hearty and warming soups   50

Chilled and refreshing salads   90

Warm and surprising salads   130

Index   172

Introduction

Delicious soups and filling salads – *Soups & Salads* is an inspiring collection of recipes from the best of Weight Watchers cookbooks. Far more than just simple soup and a dull salad, all these recipes are easy, filling and wonderfully tasty.

Soups vary from traditional favourites, such as Leek and Potato and Cream of Chicken, to delicious modern combinations like Thai Spinach and Watercress and Asparagus. There are even a couple of chilled soups – perfect for a hot summer day.

Salad is so much more than just a side dish, and these recipes prove it. Try a warm salad such as Marinated Chicken or Hot Bacon and Plum, or serve something special like Asparagus, Parma Ham and Nectarine Salad at a dinner party. There are so many combinations here – you'll never be at a loss for a soup or salad recipe again.

About Weight Watchers

For more than 40 years Weight Watchers has been helping people around the world to lose weight using a long term sustainable approach. Weight Watchers successful weight loss system is based on four tried and trusted principles:

- Eating healthily
- Being more active
- Adjusting behaviour to help weight loss
- Getting support in weekly meetings

Our unique ***ProPoints*** system empowers you to manage your food plan and make wise recipe choices for a healthier, happier you. To find out more about Weight Watchers and the ***ProPoints*** values for these recipes contact Customer Services on 0845 345 1500.

Storing and freezing

Although salads do not generally store well, you can store any leftover soup in sealed containers in the fridge and use them up within a day or two. Many of the soups in this book can also be frozen. However, it is important to make sure you know how to freeze safely.

- Wrap any food to be frozen in rigid containers or strong freezer bags. This is important to stop foods contaminating each other or getting freezer burn.
- Label the containers or bags with the contents and date – your freezer should have a star marking that tells you how long you can keep different types of frozen food.
- Never freeze warm food – always let it cool completely first.
- Never freeze food that has already been frozen and defrosted.
- Freeze food in portions, then you can take out as little or as much as you need each time.
- Defrost what you need in the fridge, making sure you put anything that might have juices, such as meat, on a covered plate or in a container.
- Fresh food, such as raw meat or fish, should be wrapped and frozen as soon as possible.
- Most fruit and vegetables can be frozen by open freezing. Lay them out on a tray, freeze until solid and then pack them into bags.
- Some vegetables, such as peas, broccoli and broad beans can be blanched first by cooking for 2 minutes in boiling water. Drain and refresh under cold water and freeze once cold.
- Fresh herbs are great frozen – either seal leaves in bags or, for soft herbs such as basil and parsley, chop finely and add to ice cube trays with water. These are great for dropping into soups straight from the freezer.

Some things cannot be frozen. Whole eggs do not freeze well, but egg yolks and whites can be frozen separately. Vegetables with a high water content, such as salad leaves, celery and cucumber, will not freeze. Fried foods will be soggy if frozen, and sauces such as mayonnaise will separate when thawed and should not be frozen.

Shopping hints and tips

Always buy the best ingredients that you can afford. If you are going to cook healthy meals, it is worth investing in some quality ingredients that will really add flavour to your dishes. When buying meat, choose lean cuts of meat or lean mince, and if you are buying prepacked cooked sliced meat, buy it fresh from the deli counter. Packaged cooked meat usually has salt and preservatives added. When choosing fruit and vegetables, look for the best fresh seasonal produce you can find.

For dressings, choose the best quality balsamic vinegar you can afford and a good quality olive oil. Try a few brands to find the one you like.

When you're going around the supermarket it's tempting to pick up foods you like and put them in your trolley without thinking about how you will use them. So, a good plan is to decide what dishes you want to cook before you go shopping, check your store cupboard and make a list of what you need. You'll save time by not drifting aimlessly around the supermarket picking up what you fancy.

We've added a checklist here for some of the store cupboard ingredients used in this book. Just add fresh ingredients in your regular shop and you'll be ready to cook any of the delicious recipes in *Soups & Salads*.

Store cupboard checklist

- artichokes, canned in water
- artificial sweetener
- bay leaves
- bouquet garni
- bulgar wheat, dried
- butter beans, canned
- capers
- chick peas, canned
- chilli (flakes and powder)
- chilli sauce
- Chinese five spice
- cinnamon, ground
- coconut milk, reduced fat
- cooking spray, calorie controlled
- coriander seeds
- coriander, ground
- cornflour
- couscous, dried
- crab meat, canned
- cumin, ground
- curry paste
- curry powder
- dressing, fat free

- fennel seeds
- fish sauce
- flour, plain
- garam masala
- gravy granules
- herbs, dried (mixed and Italian)
- honey, runny
- horseradish sauce
- kidney beans, canned
- lentils, dried
- mayonnaise, extra light
- mint sauce
- mushrooms, dried porcini
- mustard (Dijon and wholegrain)
- noodles, dried
- nutmeg
- oil (vegetable and olive)
- olives in brine, black
- paprika
- passata
- pasta (dried and fresh)
- pearl barley, dried
- peppercorns

- peppers, piquante
- pineapple, canned in natural juice
- raisins
- rice, dried brown
- salt
- sesame seeds
- soy sauce
- stock cubes
- sugar, caster
- sweetcorn, canned
- Tabasco sauce
- teriyaki sauce
- Thai 7 spice
- tomato purée
- tomatoes, canned
- tuna, canned in brine
- turmeric
- vinegar (balsamic and white wine)
- water chestnuts, canned
- Worcestershire sauce

Light and colourful soups

Thai spinach soup

Serves 4
76 calories per serving
Takes 15 minutes

**calorie controlled cooking
spray**

**2.5 cm (1 inch) fresh root
ginger, chopped finely**

4 garlic cloves, crushed

1 teaspoon Thai curry paste

**500 g (1 lb 2 oz) baby spinach
or spinach, washed, tough
stems removed and leaves
shredded**

**1.2 litres (2 pints) vegetable
stock**

**100 ml (3½ fl oz) reduced fat
coconut milk**

**salt and freshly ground black
pepper**

*A super quick and creamy soup that can be rustled up in
just 15 minutes.*

1 Heat a large saucepan and spray with the cooking spray.
Add the ginger, garlic and curry paste and stir fry for a few
minutes, until fragrant.

2 Add the spinach and stock and bring to the boil. Simmer
for a few moments and then, using a blender, or hand held
blender, liquidise the soup until smooth. You may need to do
this in batches.

3 Return to the pan to warm through, stir in the coconut milk
and season to taste. Serve in warmed bowls.

Tip... Once you have added the coconut milk to the soup
do not let it boil or the soup will split.

Variation... This soup can also be made with watercress
instead of the spinach.

Hot and sour broth

Serves 2
297 calories per serving
Takes 20 minutes
❄

200 g (7 oz) lean pork mince
1½ teaspoons yellow Thai
  curry paste
1 tablespoon finely chopped
  fresh coriander
1 spring onion, very finely
  chopped
600 ml (20 fl oz) hot chicken
  stock
1½ tablespoons rice wine
  vinegar
50 g (1¾ oz) shiitake
  mushrooms, trimmed and
  sliced
½ red chilli, de-seeded and
  sliced
50 g (1¾ oz) dried rice noodles
60 g (2 oz) sugar snap peas
salt and freshly ground black
  pepper

Spicy yet soothing, this makes a wonderful light meal.

1 Put the pork mince, curry paste, coriander and spring onion into a large bowl and mix until combined. It's best to do this with your hands. With wet hands, divide the mixture into six small balls.

2 Put the chicken stock and rice wine vinegar into a wide lidded saucepan and add the pork balls. Bring to the boil, cover and simmer for 5 minutes. Gently stir in the mushrooms, chilli and noodles. Cover and simmer for a further 3 minutes.

3 Add the sugar snap peas, cover and cook for a further 2 minutes. Season to taste and ladle into warmed bowls. Serve immediately.

Asparagus and lemon soup

Serves 2
62 calories per serving
Takes 15 minutes

275 g (9½ oz) asparagus,
  chopped roughly
1 garlic clove, chopped
600 ml (20 fl oz) hot vegetable
  stock
25 g (1 oz) low fat soft cheese
1 lemon, finely grated zest of
  ½, remaining half cut into
  wedges, to serve

Use thick slightly woody asparagus for this soup as it has a better flavour and texture when blended.

1 Place the asparagus, garlic and stock in a large saucepan, bring to the boil and simmer for 5 minutes until the asparagus is soft.

2 Using a blender, or hand held blender, liquidise the soup until smooth. You may need to do this in batches.

3 Return to the pan, stir in the soft cheese and lemon zest and warm through until hot. Serve with the lemon wedges for squeezing over.

Gazpacho

Serves 6

117 calories per serving

Takes 25 minutes +
  10 minutes soaking +
  2–3 hours chilling

2 medium slices stale bread,
  crusts removed

1 kg (2 lb 4 oz) ripe tomatoes,
  peeled and chopped

½ cucumber, chopped roughly

1 small red onion, chopped
  roughly

2 garlic cloves, crushed

1 green or red pepper,
  de-seeded and chopped

2 tablespoons olive oil

2 tablespoons white wine
  vinegar

2 tablespoons chopped fresh
  parsley

a handful of fresh basil or
  mint, plus a few leaves for
  garnish

sea salt and freshly ground
  black pepper

ice cubes, to serve

This chilled Spanish soup is fantastic on a hot day.

1 Soak the bread in water for 10 minutes, squeeze it a little and then blend in a food processor with all the remaining ingredients, except the garnish and ice cubes. Taste and check the seasoning.

2 Empty into a bowl, cover and chill in the fridge for 2–3 hours.

3 Serve chilled, garnished with the basil or mint leaves and a few ice cubes.

Variation... This soup does not have to be blended. For a chunkier version, just finely chop all the vegetables and mix with the other ingredients.

Celery, tomato and apple soup

**calorie controlled cooking
 spray**

**1 head of celery, chopped
 (reserve some leaves to
 garnish)**

2 onions, chopped

2 leeks, chopped

**2 cooking apples, peeled,
 cored and chopped**

**850 ml (1½ pints) vegetable
 stock**

**300 ml (10 fl oz) unsweetened
 apple juice**

**2 x 400 g cans chopped
 tomatoes**

**3 tablespoons chopped fresh
 parsley**

1 teaspoon caster sugar

**salt and freshly ground black
 pepper**

*This is a beautiful combination of summery flavours that is
a bit unusual and perfect for a special occasion.*

1 Heat a large non stick saucepan and spray with the cooking
spray. Add the celery, onions and leeks and cook over a medium
heat, stirring frequently, for 8–10 minutes.

2 Add the apples, stock, apple juice and tomatoes and bring up
to the boil. Reduce the heat and simmer gently for 40 minutes.

3 Using a blender, or hand held blender, liquidise the soup until
smooth. You may need to do this in batches. Return to the pan
to warm through. Add the parsley and caster sugar, season to
taste and then serve garnished with the reserved celery leaves.

Soupe au pistou

Serves 4
303 calories per serving
Takes 25 minutes to prepare,
  40 minutes to cook

calorie controlled cooking spray

1 onion, chopped

2 leeks, chopped finely

400 g can chopped tomatoes

200 g (7 oz) potatoes, peeled and diced finely

350 g (12 oz) courgettes, diced finely

2 carrots, peeled and diced finely

100 g (3½ oz) green beans, trimmed and quartered

300 g can haricot beans, drained and rinsed

50 g (1¾ oz) dried spaghettini, broken into short pieces

a bunch of fresh flat leaf parsley, chopped

salt and freshly ground black pepper

For the pistou

a bunch of fresh basil

1 large garlic clove, crushed

2 tablespoons olive oil

25 g (1 oz) Parmesan cheese, grated

35 g (1¼ oz) low fat soft cheese

This soup is full of delicious vegetables, beans and pasta. The addition of pistou, which is like pesto but without the pine nut kernels, gives it a wonderfully aromatic flavour.

1 Spray a large, lidded, non stick saucepan with the cooking spray, add the onion and leeks and cook for 2 minutes, adding a splash of water if they start to stick.

2 Add the other vegetables and haricot beans, mix everything together and then pour over 2 litres (3½ pints) of hot water. Cover and simmer for 30 minutes.

3 Meanwhile, make the pistou by whizzing the basil, garlic and oil in a food processor, or use a hand held blender, until smooth. If it is too dry, add a little water. Scrape down the jug and then add both the cheeses. Pulse quickly until mixed in.

4 Add the spaghettini, parsley and seasoning to the soup and cook for a further 10 minutes. Just before serving, stir in the pistou, saving a little to blob on top.

Chilli vegetable soup

Serves 4

187 calories per serving

Takes 25 minutes

1 tablespoon stir fry oil

a bunch of spring onions or 1 large onion, finely sliced

1 red pepper, de-seeded and finely sliced

1 yellow pepper, de-seeded and finely sliced

1 litre (1¾ pints) vegetable stock

2–3 teaspoons chilli sauce

1 teaspoon Chinese five spice

50 g (1¾ oz) dried thread egg noodles

100 g (3½ oz) marinated tofu pieces

salt and freshly ground black pepper

This is a great vegetarian version of the recipe on page 38.

1 Heat the oil in a large saucepan and add the spring onions or onion and peppers. Stir fry for 2–3 minutes.

2 Add the stock, chilli sauce, Chinese five spice and noodles. Bring up to the boil and simmer for 5 minutes, until the noodles are tender.

3 Add the tofu, cook for 2 minutes and then season. Ladle into warmed bowls and serve at once.

Tip... Stir fry oil is flavoured with garlic, ginger and spices and gives an excellent flavour to this soup but if you don't have any you could simply use vegetable oil instead.

Tortelloni and seafood broth

Serves 2
221 calories per serving
Takes 15 minutes

Full of Asian flavour, this is a tasty seafood version of the recipe on page 37.

600 ml (20 fl oz) hot fish stock
1 red chilli, sliced
1 lemongrass stem, tough leaves discarded, halved
1 carrot, peeled and cut into matchsticks
60 g (2 oz) cooked peeled tiger prawns
½ x 300 g packet fresh arrabiata tortelloni
4 spring onions, sliced finely
50 g (1¾ oz) mange tout, sliced in half on the diagonal
2 tablespoons chopped fresh coriander, to garnish

1 Put the stock, chilli and lemongrass in a large lidded saucepan and bring to the boil. Add the carrot, cover and simmer gently for 2 minutes.

2 Add the prawns and tortelloni, cover again and simmer for a further 3–4 minutes, or according to the packet instructions, until cooked. Add the spring onions and mange tout and remove from the heat.

3 Discard the lemongrass and ladle into warmed shallow bowls. Scatter over the coriander and serve immediately.

Sweet tomato and basil soup

Serves 4
83 calories per serving
Takes 15 minutes

calorie controlled cooking
   spray
1 leek, sliced
600 ml (20 fl oz) vegetable
   stock
700 g jar passata
4 tablespoons chopped fresh
   basil, plus extra leaves to
   garnish
2 teaspoons artificial
   sweetener
freshly ground black pepper
4 tablespoons very low fat
   plain fromage frais, to serve

Using passata means this soup is super quick to make.

1 Spray a large, lidded, non stick saucepan with the cooking spray. Add the leek, cover and cook for 2 minutes. Add 3 tablespoons of stock, cover again and cook for another 3 minutes until softened.

2 Pour in the rest of the stock and the passata. Season with freshly ground black pepper, cover and bring to a simmer. Cook for 5 minutes and then, using a blender, or hand held blender, liquidise the soup until smooth, adding the basil and sweetener. You may need to do this in batches.

3 Return to the pan to warm through and serve topped with the fromage frais and extra basil leaves.

Chilled cucumber and mint soup

Serves 4

120 calories per serving

Takes 25 minutes + 4 hours chilling

calorie controlled cooking spray

2 shallots, chopped finely

1 large cucumber, peeled and chopped finely

1 tablespoon plain flour

850 ml (1½ pints) vegetable stock

500 g (1 lb 2 oz) low fat natural yogurt

1 tablespoon chopped fresh mint, plus extra to garnish

salt and freshly ground black pepper

A fresh chilled soup for hot days.

1 Heat a large, lidded, non stick saucepan and spray with the cooking spray. Stir fry the shallots and cucumber for 5 minutes until softened.

2 Sprinkle in the flour and then gradually add the stock, stirring continuously. Season, cover and simmer for 10 minutes.

3 Using a blender, or hand held blender, liquidise the soup until smooth. You may need to do this in batches. Leave until cool and then stir in the yogurt and mint. (Do not add the yogurt to the mixture while it is hot as the yogurt may separate.) Chill for at least 4 hours before serving, garnished with the extra mint leaves.

Carrot and spinach soup

Serves 4
125 calories per serving
Takes 30 minutes

❄ (before adding milk or yogurt)

calorie controlled cooking spray
1 large onion, chopped
1 garlic clove, crushed
600 g (1 lb 5 oz) carrots, peeled and sliced roughly
1 litre (1¾ pints) vegetable stock
4 tablespoons low fat natural yogurt
1 teaspoon freshly grated nutmeg
200 ml (7 fl oz) skimmed milk
30 g (1¼ oz) spinach, washed and shredded finely
salt and freshly ground black pepper

The contrast between the green spinach and the orange carrot makes this soup particularly attractive, and it tastes as good as it looks.

1 Spray a large, lidded, non stick saucepan with the cooking spray, add the onion and garlic and cook gently for a few minutes to soften but not brown.

2 Add the carrots and stock. Bring to the boil, season and simmer, covered, for 15 minutes or until the carrots are cooked through. Meanwhile, mix the yogurt with half the nutmeg and put to one side.

3 Using a blender, or hand held blender, liquidise the soup until smooth. You may need to do this in batches. Return to the pan, stir in the milk and the rest of the nutmeg and heat. Meanwhile, warm four bowls.

4 Once the soup is reheated, remove from the heat and stir in the spinach. Check the seasoning and pour into the warmed bowls, topping each with a swirl of the nutmeg flavoured yogurt.

Tip... Since you are going to liquidise the soup, there's no need to chop the carrots and onions for this recipe 'neatly' as the shapes and sizes really don't matter.

Variation... For a herby carrot soup, replace the spinach with chopped fresh parsley or coriander.

Watercress and asparagus soup

Serves 4
49 calories per serving
Takes 25 minutes

900 ml (1½ pints) vegetable stock
1 baby cauliflower, chopped roughly
350 g (12 oz) asparagus spears, chopped
4 spring onions, chopped
50 g (1¾ oz) watercress
25 g packet fresh mint, leaves only
salt and freshly ground black pepper

This smooth, velvety soup is very refreshing in the summer yet wonderfully comforting on a winter's day. Serve with 2 x 15 g (½ oz) wholewheat crispbreads and 1 tablespoon of 0% fat Greek yogurt per person.

1 Put the stock and cauliflower in a large saucepan and bring to the boil. Add the asparagus and spring onions, bring back to the boil and then simmer for 3 minutes. Take off the heat and stir in the watercress and mint until wilted. Leave to cool for 5–10 minutes.

2 Using a blender, or hand held blender, liquidise the soup until smooth. You may need to do this in batches. Return to the pan to warm through if necessary, check the seasoning and serve immediately in warmed bowls.

Spicy tortelloni broth

Serves 2
195 calories per serving
Takes 15 minutes

600 ml (20 fl oz) hot vegetable
stock
1 red chilli, sliced
1 lemongrass stem, tough
leaves discarded, halved
1 carrot, peeled and cut into
matchsticks
½ x 300 g packet fresh
arrabiata tortelloni
4 spring onions, sliced finely
50 g (1¾ oz) mange tout,
sliced in half on the diagonal
2 tablespoons chopped fresh
coriander, to garnish

*Infused with chilli and lemongrass, this soup is sure to
blow the winter blues away.*

1 Put the vegetable stock, chilli and lemongrass in a large
lidded saucepan and bring to the boil. Add the carrot, cover
and simmer gently for 2 minutes.

2 Add the tortelloni, cover again and simmer for a further
3–4 minutes, or according to the packet instructions, until
cooked. Add the spring onions and mange tout and remove
from the heat.

3 Discard the lemongrass and ladle into warmed shallow
bowls. Scatter over the coriander and serve immediately.

Variation... For a zingy seafood variation, see the recipe
on page 27.

Chilli prawn soup

Serves 4
155 calories per serving
Takes 25 minutes

1 tablespoon stir fry oil

a bunch of spring onions or 1 large onion, finely sliced

1 red pepper, de-seeded and finely sliced

1 yellow pepper, de-seeded and finely sliced

1 litre (1¾ pints) chicken stock

2–3 teaspoons chilli sauce

1 teaspoon Chinese five spice

50 g (1¾ oz) dried thread egg noodles

100 g (3½ oz) cooked peeled prawns, defrosted if frozen

salt and freshly ground black pepper

Enjoy a wonderful bowl of this spicy soup for supper with a 50 g (1¾ oz) brown roll per person.

1 Heat the oil in a large saucepan and add the spring onions or onion and peppers. Stir fry for 2–3 minutes.

2 Add the stock, chilli sauce, Chinese five spice and noodles. Bring up to the boil and simmer for 5 minutes, until the noodles are tender.

3 Add the prawns, cook for 2 minutes and then season. Ladle into warmed bowls and serve at once.

Tip... Stir fry oil is flavoured with garlic, ginger and spices and gives an excellent flavour to this soup but if you don't have any you could simply use vegetable oil instead.

Variations... Try using 50 g (1¾ oz) of dried rice instead of noodles.

Ⓥ For a wonderful vegetarian version, see the recipe on page 26.

Creamy carrot and orange soup

Serves 4

162 calories per serving

Takes 25 minutes

❄

1.2 litres (2 pints) vegetable stock

500 g (1 lb 2 oz) carrots, peeled and grated coarsely

400 g (14 oz) parsnips, peeled and grated coarsely

finely grated zest and juice of an orange

2 tablespoons half fat crème fraîche

salt and freshly ground black pepper

A hint of orange brings out the natural sweetness of the root vegetables in this heart-warming soup.

1 In a large lidded saucepan, bring the stock to the boil. Add the grated vegetables and orange zest and juice. Season to taste.

2 Cover and simmer for 15 minutes until the vegetables are tender.

3 Remove from the heat and add the crème fraîche. Using a blender, or hand held blender, liquidise the soup until smooth. You may need to do this in batches. Return to the pan to warm through and serve in warmed bowls.

Pea, mint and ham soup

Serves 4
228 calories per serving
Takes 20 minutes

calorie controlled cooking spray
2 onions, chopped finely
2 garlic cloves, crushed
1 soft leaved lettuce, sliced
a small bunch of fresh mint
500 g (1 lb 2 oz) fresh or frozen and defrosted peas
a pinch of sugar
850 ml (1½ pints) chicken or vegetable stock
4 tablespoons half fat crème fraîche
salt and freshly ground black pepper

To garnish
4 thin slices Parma ham
fresh chives, chopped, to garnish (optional)

A modern version of the classic pea and ham soup, this is a vibrant pea-green soup garnished with crispy curls of grilled Parma ham.

1 Heat a large non stick saucepan and spray with the cooking spray. Add the onions and garlic and cook for 4 minutes until softened.

2 Add all the other ingredients except the crème fraîche and garnish. Bring to the boil and simmer for 2 minutes.

3 Meanwhile, preheat the grill to medium-high, line the grill pan with foil and grill the Parma ham until crispy.

4 Using a blender, or hand held blender, liquidise the soup until smooth. You may need to do this in batches. Return to the pan to warm through. Check the seasoning and stir in the crème fraîche. Serve garnished with the grilled Parma ham and sprinkled with fresh chives, if using.

Variation... If you don't have Parma ham, grill 2 x 25 g (1 oz) lean back bacon rashers until very crispy and then chop and sprinkle over.

Winter greens soup

Serves 4
218 calories per serving
Takes 25 minutes
❄ (soup only)

**calorie controlled cooking
  spray**
1 leek, sliced
**½ small cauliflower, cut into
  small florets**
**3 ripe pears, peeled, cored and
  chopped**
**1 litre (1¾ pints) hot vegetable
  stock**
**½ Savoy cabbage, outer
  leaves removed, cored and
  shredded**
**8 x 15 g (½ oz) slices Parma
  ham**
8 x 5 g thin breadsticks
**175 g (6 oz) frozen peas,
  defrosted**
**salt and freshly ground black
  pepper**

*Served with breadsticks wrapped with ham, this really is
sophisticated comfort food.*

1 Preheat the oven to Gas Mark 6/200°C/fan oven 180°C.
Spray a large, lidded, non stick saucepan with the cooking
spray and add the leek, cauliflower and pears. Cover and
cook gently for 5 minutes, stirring occasionally.

2 Add the hot stock and bring to the boil. Add the cabbage,
turn down the heat, cover and simmer for 5 minutes until
the vegetables are tender.

3 Meanwhile, wrap a slice of Parma ham around each
breadstick and put on a non stick baking tray. Bake in the
oven for 8–10 minutes until crispy. Remove and leave to
go cold.

4 Add the peas to the soup and, using a blender, or hand
held blender, liquidise the soup until smooth. You may need
to do this in batches. Return to the pan to warm through,
season and serve with the Parma ham breadsticks.

Ⓥ **Variation...** You can replace the Parma ham with
8 x 8 g (¼ oz) Quorn Deli Ham Style Slices and bake as
above.

Chicken pasta soup

Serves 4
394 calories per serving
Takes 20 minutes

calorie controlled cooking
  spray
2 onions, sliced thinly
2 garlic cloves, crushed
150 g (5½ oz) cooked skinless
  boneless chicken breast
2 litres (3½ pints) chicken
  stock
300 g (10½ oz) dried spaghetti
  or spaghettini, broken up
salt and freshly ground black
  pepper

This soup has wonderful comforting qualities. It's also a great way to use up leftover chicken.

1 Heat a large, lidded, non stick saucepan, spray with the cooking spray and add the onions and garlic. Stir fry for 2 minutes, turn down the heat, cover and leave the onions and garlic to sweat for 10 minutes.

2 Add the chicken and stock and bring to the boil.

3 Add the pasta and simmer for 10 minutes. Check the seasoning and serve in warmed bowls.

Tip... To make a good fresh chicken stock, simply take a leftover chicken carcass, remove any meat and reserve. Place the carcass in a large saucepan with a roughly chopped carrot, onion and celery stick, a couple of peeled and crushed garlic cloves, a bay leaf and some rosemary or thyme. Cover with water and simmer for 1½–2 hours, occasionally skimming off the fat with a spoon. Strain and keep in the fridge.

Red hot tomato and beetroot soup

Serves 4

102 calories per serving

Takes 10 minutes to prepare,
30 minutes to cook

calorie controlled cooking
spray

1 large onion, chopped

1 garlic clove, crushed

225 g (8 oz) raw beetroot,
grated or finely sliced

225 g (8 oz) tomatoes, skinned
and roughly chopped

300 ml (10 fl oz) tomato juice

1 tablespoon tomato purée

1 teaspoon ground cumin

½ teaspoon ground cinnamon

600 ml (20 fl oz) hot vegetable
stock

salt and freshly ground black
pepper

To serve

4 tablespoons low fat natural
yogurt

soy sauce

*A vibrant blend of tomatoes and beetroot with a hint
of cumin, this soup looks really attractive – perfect for
entertaining.*

1 Heat a large, lidded, non stick saucepan and spray with the
cooking spray. Add the onion, garlic and beetroot. Cover and
cook gently for 10 minutes, shaking the pan occasionally.

2 Add the tomatoes, tomato juice, tomato purée, spices and
stock. Cover and bring to the boil. Reduce the heat and simmer
gently for 15 minutes or until the vegetables are tender. Season
well.

3 Using a blender, or hand held blender, liquidise the soup until
smooth. You may need to do this in batches. Return to the pan
to warm through. Adjust the seasoning to taste and ladle into
warmed bowls. Serve immediately, topping each bowl with a
tablespoon of yogurt and a drizzle of soy sauce.

Tips... To skin fresh tomatoes, put them in a bowl, cover
with boiling water for a few minutes and then drain and
leave to cool slightly. Use a small knife to peel off the skin,
which should come away from the flesh easily.

For convenience, replace the fresh tomatoes and tomato
juice with a 400 g can of chopped tomatoes.

Variation... For a fruity note, add 1 cooking apple, peeled,
cored and chopped, with the tomatoes and garnish with
fine slices of a red skinned dessert apple.

Butternut squash soup

Serves 2

87 calories per serving

Takes 10 minutes to prepare,
20 minutes to cook

1 small butternut squash,
peeled, de-seeded and
chopped

1 onion, chopped

600 ml (20 fl oz) hot vegetable
stock

½ teaspoon ground cumin

½ tablespoon ground
coriander

salt and freshly ground black
pepper

1 tablespoon chopped fresh
parsley, to garnish

Butternut squash has a sweet creamy texture, perfect for soup.

1 Put the squash and onion into a large lidded saucepan and add the stock and spices.

2 Bring to the boil, cover, reduce the heat and simmer for about 20 minutes until the squash is tender.

3 Using a blender, or hand held blender, liquidise the soup until smooth. You may need to do this in batches.

4 Return to the saucepan and reheat gently. Season to taste and serve in warmed bowls garnished with the parsley.

Hearty and warming soups

Chicken and vegetable chowder

Serves 2

352 calories per serving

Takes 15 minutes to prepare,
35–40 minutes to cook

❄

**165 g (5¾ oz) skinless
boneless chicken breast,
diced**

**425 ml (15 fl oz) chicken or
vegetable stock**

2 carrots, peeled and grated

2 leeks, sliced

½ swede, peeled and diced

**2 tablespoons dried yellow
lentils, rinsed**

**300 ml (10 fl oz) semi
skimmed milk**

**2 tablespoons fresh, frozen
or canned sweetcorn**

**salt and freshly ground black
pepper**

*Cook this soup, pop it in the freezer and then enjoy it when
you don't have time to prepare meals.*

1 Place all the ingredients except the milk, sweetcorn and
seasoning in a large saucepan and bring to the boil.

2 Turn down the heat, simmer for 25–30 minutes and then
add the milk and sweetcorn. Season and warm through for
a further 10 minutes on a gentle heat before serving.

Manhattan seafood soup

Serves 4

216 calories per serving

Takes 15 minutes to prepare,
30 minutes to cook.

**calorie controlled cooking
spray**

**2 x 25 g (1 oz) lean smoked
back bacon rashers,
chopped**

1 onion, chopped finely

**1 green pepper, de-seeded and
chopped**

2 celery sticks, diced

**700 ml (1¼ pints) vegetable
or fish stock**

400 g can chopped tomatoes

**300 g (10½ oz) potatoes,
peeled and diced**

**400 g (14 oz) frozen mixed
seafood, defrosted**

**salt and freshly ground black
pepper**

*A meal-in-a-bowl type of soup, this makes for a hearty
lunch or light meal.*

1 Spray a large, lidded, non stick saucepan with the cooking
spray and fry the bacon over a high heat for 2 minutes until
lightly browned.

2 Add the onion, green pepper and celery and stir fry for
5 minutes, until beginning to soften. Add a splash of the stock
if needed to stop the vegetables from sticking and scorching.

3 Stir in the tomatoes, potatoes and remaining stock. Season,
cover, bring to a simmer and cook for 15–20 minutes or until
the potatoes are tender.

4 Stir in the seafood and heat for 2–3 minutes. Ladle into
warmed deep bowls or mugs to serve.

Butter bean and bacon soup

Serves 4
212 calories per serving
Takes 15 minutes
❄

1 onion, chopped finely
2 garlic cloves, crushed
1 teaspoon dried rosemary
850 ml (1½ pints) chicken stock
calorie controlled cooking spray
4 x 25 g (1 oz) lean smoked back bacon rashers, cut into small strips
3 x 410 g cans butter beans, drained and rinsed
freshly ground black pepper

A flavoursome soup that will keep you satisfied for hours after.

1 Put the onion, garlic, rosemary and 150 ml (5 fl oz) of the stock in a large lidded saucepan. Cover, bring to the boil and simmer briskly for 5 minutes until softened.

2 Meanwhile, spray a non stick frying pan with the cooking spray and fry the bacon for 2–3 minutes until browned and crisp. Set aside.

3 Stir the beans and the rest of the stock into the saucepan. Cover, bring back to the boil and simmer for 3 minutes. Using a blender, or hand held blender, liquidise the soup until smooth. You may need to do this in batches.

4 Return to the pan to warm through and season with freshly ground black pepper to taste. Ladle into warmed bowls and serve topped with the crispy bacon bits.

🅥 **Variation...** For a vegetarian version, replace the bacon with 4 Quorn Deli Bacon Style Rashers, and use vegetable stock in place of chicken stock.

Middle Eastern lentil soup

Serves 6

227 calories per serving

Takes 5 minutes to prepare,
40 minutes to cook

calorie controlled cooking
spray

1 large onion, chopped

1 celery stick, with leaves,
chopped

1 large carrot, peeled and
chopped

350 g (12 oz) dried lentils
(see Tip)

2 litres (3½ pints) vegetable
stock

juice of ½ a lemon

1 teaspoon ground cumin

salt and freshly ground black
pepper

*Hearty, quick and easy to prepare, this soup is full of
warming flavours.*

1 Heat a large, lidded, non stick saucepan and spray with the
cooking spray. Add the onion, celery and carrot and stir fry for
5 minutes until softened, adding a splash of water if they start
to stick.

2 Add the lentils and stock and bring to the boil. Skim off any
froth that rises to the surface, cover and simmer gently for
about 30 minutes until the lentils are soft – the cooking time
depends on the type and age of the lentils used.

3 When the lentils are cooked, add the lemon juice, cumin and
seasoning. Using a blender, or hand held blender, liquidise the
soup until smooth. You may need to do this in batches. Return
to the pan to warm through and serve in warmed bowls.

Tip... Any type of lentil works in this recipe, but the red
ones are good for their colour and fluffy texture.

Golden onion soup

Serves 6

75 calories per serving

Takes 10 minutes to prepare,
35 minutes to cook

calorie controlled cooking
spray

600 g (1 lb 5 oz) onions,
halved and sliced finely

1 teaspoon granulated sugar

175 g (6 oz) potatoes, peeled
and diced

1.2 litres (2 pints) hot
vegetable or chicken stock

1 tablespoon chopped fresh
thyme or 1 teaspoon dried
thyme, plus extra sprigs to
garnish (optional)

salt and freshly ground black
pepper

For a main meal, serve topped with 2 tablespoons of grated
half fat Cheddar cheese and a 2.5 cm (1 inch) slice of
French bread per person.

1 Spray a large, lidded, non stick saucepan with the cooking
spray, add the onions and sugar and cook over a low heat for
12–15 minutes, stirring frequently, until the onions are golden.

2 Add the potatoes, half the stock and the thyme. Season and
bring to a simmer. Cover and cook for 15 minutes or until the
potatoes are tender.

3 Use a slotted spoon to remove some of the cooked onions
for a nice texture if desired. Using a blender, or hand held
blender, liquidise the remaining soup until smooth. You may
need to do this in batches. Return to the pan to warm through
with the reserved onions and remaining stock. Adjust the
seasoning to taste.

4 Serve the soup garnished with the extra thyme, if using.

Tip... Take your time to cook the onions carefully and
slowly in step 1, as the natural sugars in the onions will
slowly caramelise.

Variation... If you prefer, replace the thyme with snipped
fresh chives.

Leek and potato soup

Serves 2

83 calories per serving

Takes 15 minutes to prepare,
30 minutes to cook

1 teaspoon sunflower oil

225 g (8 oz) leeks, sliced

225 g (8 oz) potatoes, peeled
and diced

1 garlic clove, crushed

600 ml (20 fl oz) vegetable
stock

100 ml (3½ fl oz) skimmed
milk

salt and freshly ground black
pepper

A classic. You could blend the entire soup so it is completely smooth if you prefer.

1 Heat the oil in a large, lidded, non stick saucepan and add the leeks, potatoes and garlic. Cook over a gentle heat for 2–3 minutes, stirring occasionally.

2 Add the stock to the pan and bring to the boil. Reduce the heat, cover and simmer for 25 minutes.

3 Using a blender, or hand held blender, liquidise half the soup until smooth. Return the blended soup to the pan and add the milk and seasoning. Heat through and serve the soup in warmed bowls.

French broccoli and butter bean soup

Serves 2

271 calories per serving

Takes 20 minutes to prepare,
15 minutes to cook

300 g (10½ oz) broccoli,
broken into florets

1 onion, chopped

3 garlic cloves, crushed

1 tablespoon dried herbes de
Provence

850 ml (1½ pints) vegetable
stock

200 g can butter beans,
drained and rinsed

salt and freshly ground black
pepper

2 x 5 cm (2 inch) slices French
bread, to serve

This is a delicious soup with just a hint of French flavour.

1 Place the broccoli, onion, garlic, herbs and stock in a saucepan, season and bring to the boil. Turn down the heat and simmer for 15 minutes, until the broccoli is tender.

2 Using a blender, or hand held blender, liquidise the soup with the butter beans until smooth. You may need to do this in batches. Return to the pan to warm through, check the seasoning and serve in warmed bowls with a slice of French bread.

Variations... If you are not keen on broccoli, you can make this soup with 300 g (10½ oz) of chopped mushrooms instead.

For a dinner party, try making a creamy version by adding 1 tablespoon of half fat crème fraîche to each bowl.

Parsnip, ham and apple soup

Serves 2

369 calories per serving

Takes 15 minutes to prepare,
45 minutes to cook

❄

calorie controlled cooking
spray

1 large onion, chopped roughly

500 g (1lb 2 oz) parsnips,
peeled and chopped roughly

1 cooking apple, peeled, cored
and chopped roughly

1.5 litres (2¾ pints) vegetable
stock

150 ml (5 fl oz) skimmed milk
or soya milk

100 g (3½ oz) lean ham,
chopped

salt and freshly ground black
pepper

*The addition of apple gives this soup a sweet edge that
enhances the intense soothing parsnip flavour.*

1 Spray a large, lidded, non stick saucepan with the cooking
spray, add the onion and stir fry for 3 minutes, until softened
and golden, adding a splash of water if it starts to stick.

2 Add the parsnips, apple and vegetable stock to the pan.
Bring to the boil and simmer for 45 minutes, covered.

3 Using a blender, or hand held blender, liquidise the soup
until smooth and then stir in the milk. You may need to do this
in batches. Return to the pan, add the ham and warm through.
Check the seasoning and serve in warmed bowls.

Tip... Make soups into an instant snack or lunch by
preparing them in advance and freezing. Make a large
batch by multiplying up the recipe quantities, measure
the soup out into portions and freeze. When you are
ready to eat, simply take it out of the freezer and pop
in the microwave or gently thaw on the hob for a quick,
wholesome and satisfying filler.

Chicken and vegetable broth

Serves 4

350 calories per serving

Takes 10 minutes to prepare,
  1 hour to cook

❄

calorie controlled cooking
  spray
1 large onion, sliced finely
2 large carrots, peeled and cut
  into 1 cm (½ inch) slices
2 celery sticks, sliced
250 g (9 oz) swede, peeled and
  cut into chunks
65 g (2½ oz) dried pearl barley
500 g (1 lb 2 oz) chicken
  thighs, skinless but on
  the bone
1.5 litres (2¾ pints) hot
  chicken or vegetable stock
350 g (12 oz) mushrooms,
  sliced thickly
1 teaspoon dried sage or
  1 tablespoon finely chopped
  fresh sage
2 tablespoons cornflour
2 teaspoons Worcestershire
  sauce
salt and freshly ground black
  pepper
2 tablespoons chopped fresh
  parsley, to serve

*Enjoy this mighty main meal soup with the family for a
midweek supper or Saturday lunch.*

1 Spray a large, lidded, non stick saucepan with the cooking
spray. Add the onion, carrots, celery and swede and stir fry
for 5 minutes until slightly softened. Add the pearl barley and
chicken thighs and stir fry for 3–4 minutes, or until the chicken
is lightly coloured.

2 Add the stock and bring to the boil, lower the heat, cover and
simmer gently for 35–40 minutes. During this time the barley
will swell and soften, absorbing some of the stock.

3 Use tongs to remove the cooked chicken to a chopping board.
Add the mushrooms and sage to the saucepan and continue
to simmer, uncovered, for 10 minutes. Meanwhile, remove the
chicken from the bones and roughly shred. Return the meat to
the saucepan. Season well to taste.

4 Blend the cornflour to a paste with the Worcestershire sauce
and a drop of cold water. Stir into the broth and continue to heat
through until the broth thickens slightly. Check the seasoning.

5 Ladle into warmed bowls, scatter over the parsley and serve
immediately.

Tips... Dark-gilled open mushrooms will add more flavour
and depth to this broth than button mushrooms, so look
out for those.

Spicy fish soup

Serves 4
262 calories per serving
Takes 30 minutes

1 tablespoon vegetable oil
1 large onion, sliced finely
2 leeks, sliced finely
1 large carrot, peeled and
   grated
2 garlic cloves, crushed, or
   1 teaspoon garlic purée
1 teaspoon turmeric
1 teaspoon ground cumin
1 teaspoon garam masala
75 g (2¾ oz) dried red lentils
400 g can chopped tomatoes
1.2 litres (2 pints) hot
   vegetable stock
400 g (14 oz) cod fillets, cut
   into chunks
juice of 2 limes
2 tablespoons chopped fresh
   coriander
salt

Deliciously warm and welcoming on a chilly night, this soup is for the whole family to enjoy. If there is any left over, take it to work as a great midday 'pick me up'. Serve with a 50 g (1¾ oz) bread roll per person.

1 Heat a large, lidded, non stick saucepan, add the oil, onion, leeks, carrot and garlic and cook for 2–3 minutes. Add the spices and lentils and stir fry for a further minute.

2 Stir in the tomatoes and hot stock. Bring to the boil, cover and simmer for 15 minutes.

3 Add the fish, lime juice and coriander and continue to cook with the lid on for a further 5 minutes. Check the seasoning. Ladle into warmed deep bowls to serve.

Tip... If you have one, use the slicing attachment on a food processor or mandolin to make swift work of preparing the vegetables.

Variation... Replace the cod with a 200 g drained can of tuna in brine and 200 g (7 oz) of cooked prawns.

Moroccan turkey soup

Serves 4

267 calories per serving

Takes 15 minutes to prepare,
30 minutes to cook

❄ (before the final step)

**calorie controlled cooking
spray**
1 onion, chopped finely
2 garlic cloves, crushed
**1 green chilli, de-seeded and
diced**
225 g (8 oz) turkey mince
1 teaspoon ground cinnamon
1 teaspoon ground cumin
½ teaspoon ground coriander
**1.2 litres (2 pints) chicken
stock**
**410 g can chick peas, drained
and rinsed**
3 tablespoons tomato purée
50 g (1¾ oz) dried couscous
**3 tablespoons chopped fresh
mint**
juice of a large lemon

*A cross between a soup and a stew, this Moroccan delight
will satisfy all of your senses. If you want the soup to taste
really authentic, add a dash of fiery Tabasco sauce before
serving.*

1 Heat a large, lidded, non stick saucepan and spray with the
cooking spray. Add the onion and brown for 5 minutes, adding
a splash of water if it starts to stick.

2 Add the garlic, chilli and turkey and cook, stirring to break
up the mince, until lightly coloured.

3 Mix in the ground spices and cook for 30 seconds before
adding the chicken stock, chick peas and tomato purée.
Bring to the boil, cover and simmer for 20 minutes.

4 Remove from the heat and stir in the couscous, mint and
lemon juice. Cover the pan and leave to stand for 5 minutes
until the couscous is tender. Ladle into warmed bowls to serve.

🅥 **Variation...** For a vegetarian version of this soup, replace
the turkey mince with Quorn mince and use vegetable
stock instead of chicken stock.

Bacon, leek and potato soup

Serves 4
225 calories per serving
Takes 25 minutes
❄

calorie controlled cooking spray
500 g (1 lb 2 oz) leeks, sliced
3 carrots, peeled and sliced
2 celery sticks, sliced
450 g (1 lb) potatoes, peeled and cut into bite size chunks
1.2 litres (2 pints) vegetable or chicken stock
2 bouquet garni
2 bay leaves
5 x 25 g (1 oz) lean back bacon rashers
4 tablespoons skimmed milk
salt and freshly ground black pepper

Leaving half the soup chunky gives it a lovely texture.

1 Heat a large, lidded, non stick saucepan and spray with the cooking spray. Add the leeks, carrots, celery and potatoes and cook for 5 minutes, stirring occasionally.

2 Add the stock, bouquet garni and bay leaves. Bring to the boil and then reduce the heat and simmer, half covered, for 15 minutes or until the vegetables are tender.

3 Meanwhile, preheat the grill to medium-high and cover the grill rack with foil. Grill the bacon until crisp and then break into pieces. Set aside.

4 Remove the bouquet garni and bay leaves from the vegetables and, using a blender, or hand held blender, liquidise half the soup until smooth. Return to the pan to warm through with the other half of the soup, season and stir in the skimmed milk.

5 Sprinkle over the bacon pieces and serve in warmed bowls.

Cream of chicken soup

Serves 4

143 calories per serving

Takes 10 minutes to prepare,
   45 minutes to cook

❄

1 tablespoon low fat spread
1 onion, chopped finely
1 leek, sliced finely
3 celery sticks, chopped
1 parsnip, peeled and chopped
250 g (9 oz) chicken leg
   quarter, skinned
1.2 litres (2 pints) hot chicken
   or vegetable stock
100 g (3½ oz) very low fat
   plain fromage frais
2 tablespoons chopped fresh
   parsley
salt and freshly ground black
   pepper

*Comforting and delicious, a bowlful of this chicken soup
will really lift your spirits.*

1 Melt the low fat spread in a large lidded saucepan and
gently sauté the onion, leek, celery and parsnip until softened;
about 10 minutes.

2 Add the chicken to the saucepan with the hot stock. Bring
to the boil, reduce the heat, cover and simmer gently for
30 minutes.

3 Using a slotted spoon, lift the chicken from the saucepan
and put it on a chopping board. Let it cool down for a few
minutes and then use two forks to strip off all the meat.
Discard the bones.

4 Transfer the soup to a blender, or use a hand held blender,
and add half the chicken and all the fromage frais. Blend for
about 15–20 seconds until smooth. Return the soup to the
saucepan, add the parsley and remaining chicken and reheat
gently.

5 Season to taste, ladle into warmed soup bowls and serve
at once.

Tip... Cooking the chicken leg in the stock gives the soup
extra flavour.

Variation... For a vegetarian version, see the recipe on
page 84.

Celeriac and butter bean soup

Serves 2
132 calories per serving
Takes 30 minutes

150 g (5½ oz) celeriac, peeled
  and chopped
1 garlic clove, crushed
600 ml (20 fl oz) vegetable
  stock
1 teaspoon fennel seeds
400 g can butter beans,
  drained and rinsed

Celeriac makes this soup thick and creamy and lends a subtle celery flavour.

1 Place the celeriac, garlic and stock in a lidded saucepan. Bring to the boil, cover and simmer for 10–12 minutes until tender.

2 Meanwhile, dry fry the fennel seeds in a small frying pan until aromatic to release their full flavour.

3 Add half the beans and, using a blender, or hand held blender, liquidise the soup until smooth. Return to the pan with the remaining beans and heat through for 2–3 minutes until hot.

4 Sprinkle over the fennel seeds before serving in warmed bowls.

Mulligatawny soup

Serves 6

88 calories per serving

Takes 20 minutes to prepare,
35 minutes to cook

1 cooking apple, cored and
chopped

2 carrots, peeled and chopped

2 leeks, sliced

1 onion, chopped

200 g (7 oz) potatoes, peeled
and diced

2 garlic cloves, crushed

1 tablespoon medium curry
powder

400 g can chopped tomatoes

1.2 litres (2 pints) hot
vegetable stock

salt and freshly ground black
pepper

For a fabulous finish, swirl 1 tablespoon of half fat crème fraîche through each portion and sprinkle with chopped fresh coriander.

1 Put the apple and all the vegetables except the tomatoes into a large non stick saucepan. Add 3 tablespoons of cold water and cook over a medium heat for about 5 minutes, until the onion looks transparent.

2 Add the garlic and curry powder and cook for another 1–2 minutes, adding a splash of water if they start to stick.

3 Add the tomatoes and stock to the saucepan. Bring up to the boil, reduce the heat and simmer for 25–30 minutes until the vegetables are soft.

4 Using a blender, or hand held blender, liquidise the soup until smooth. You may need to do this in batches. Return to the pan to warm through, season to taste and then serve in warmed bowls.

Main meal minestrone

Serves 4

264 calories per serving

Takes 15 minutes to prepare,
30 minutes to cook

❄

225 g (8 oz) extra lean beef
mince

1 teaspoon paprika

175 g (6 oz) carrots, peeled
and diced

1 red pepper, de-seeded and
chopped

1 onion, chopped

1 garlic clove, crushed

225 g (8 oz) courgettes,
chopped

400 g can chopped tomatoes

850 ml (1½ pints) beef stock

100 g (3½ oz) dried small
pasta shapes or quick cook
macaroni

2 tablespoons chopped fresh
flat leaf parsley

salt and freshly ground black
pepper

*Almost a mini casserole, this delicious soup is sure to fill
you up.*

1 Heat a large, lidded, non stick saucepan, add the beef and
dry fry until evenly browned. Stir in the paprika, carrots, red
pepper, onion, garlic and courgettes and cook for 2 minutes.

2 Stir in the tomatoes and stock and bring to the boil. Reduce
the heat, cover and simmer for 15 minutes.

3 Add the pasta and season to taste. Cook for 10 minutes
more or until the pasta is tender. Stir in the parsley and serve
the soup in four warmed bowls.

Variation... Use turkey or pork mince as an alternative
to beef, but remember to change the type of stock you
use too.

Soothing chicken soup

Serves 2

247 calories per serving

Takes 20 minutes to prepare,
40 minutes to cook

**calorie controlled cooking
spray**

1 garlic clove, crushed

**150 g (5½ oz) skinless
boneless chicken breast,
cut into strips**

2 leeks, chopped

**1 carrot, peeled and cut into
fine strips**

**a few leaves of cabbage (e.g.
Savoy) or spinach, washed
and shredded**

50 g (1¾ oz) dried brown rice

600 ml (20 fl oz) chicken stock

**salt and freshly ground black
pepper**

*Chicken with rice and vegetables makes for a soothing
soup.*

1 Spray a large, lidded, non stick saucepan with the cooking
spray, add the garlic and chicken and stir fry until browned.

2 Add the vegetables, rice and stock. Stir together, cover and
bring to the boil.

3 Reduce the heat and simmer for 35 minutes. Season to taste
and serve in warmed bowls.

Brie and courgette soup

Serves 4

190 calories per serving

Takes 15 minutes to prepare,
15 minutes to cook

❄

**200 g (7 oz) potatoes, peeled
and diced**

**300 g (10½ oz) courgettes,
halved lengthways and
sliced**

**150 g (5½ oz) leek, halved
lengthways and sliced**

**850 ml (1½ pints) vegetable
stock**

½ teaspoon dried thyme

**140 g (5 oz) Brie, rind removed
and diced**

freshly ground black pepper

An unusual creamy soup that is rich and filling.

1 Put all the ingredients, except the Brie and seasoning, into a large lidded saucepan.

2 Bring to the boil, cover and simmer for 12–15 minutes, until the vegetables are tender.

3 Add the Brie and stir until the cheese melts – do not overcook at this stage, this should only take 1–2 minutes.

4 Using a blender, or hand held blender, liquidise the soup until smooth. You may need to do this in batches. Return to the pan to warm through, season with black pepper and serve in warmed bowls.

Variation... This soup can also be made by substituting mozzarella cheese for the Brie.

Cream of vegetable soup

Serves 4

88 calories per serving

Takes 10 minutes to prepare,
45 minutes to cook

❄

1 tablespoon low fat spread
1 onion, chopped finely
1 leek, sliced finely
3 celery sticks, chopped
1 parsnip, peeled and chopped
2 carrots, peeled and chopped
1.2 litres (2 pints) hot
vegetable stock
100 g (3½ oz) very low fat
plain fromage frais
2 tablespoons chopped fresh
parsley
salt and freshly ground black
pepper

This is a soothing variation of the chicken soup on page 74.

1 Melt the low fat spread in a large, lidded, non stick saucepan and gently sauté the onion, leek, celery, parsnip and carrots until softened, about 10 minutes.

2 Add the hot stock to the saucepan, bring to the boil and then reduce the heat. Cover and simmer gently for 30 minutes.

3 Transfer the soup to a blender, or use a hand held blender, and add the fromage frais. Blend for about 15–20 seconds until smooth. Return the soup to the saucepan, add the parsley and reheat gently.

4 Season to taste, ladle into warmed soup bowls and serve at once.

Mushroom and garlic soup

Serves 2

164 calories per serving

Takes 15 minutes to prepare
+ 20 minutes soaking,
35 minutes to cook

15 g (½ oz) dried porcini
mushrooms

300 ml (10 fl oz) boiling water

1 tablespoon sunflower oil

100 g (3½ oz) shallots,
chopped

1 garlic clove, crushed

125 g (4½ oz) brown cap
mushrooms, diced

125 g (4½ oz) shiitake
mushrooms, sliced

300 ml (10 fl oz) vegetable
stock

1 tablespoon cornflour

2 tablespoons chopped fresh
parsley

salt and freshly ground black
pepper

Dried porcini mushrooms are widely available in supermarkets; their intense flavour makes them a good addition to soups, stocks and casseroles.

1 Using a pair of scissors, snip the dried mushrooms into small pieces and place them in a bowl. Pour over the boiling water and leave to stand for 20 minutes. Drain the mushrooms, reserving the liquid.

2 Meanwhile, heat the oil in a large, lidded, non stick saucepan and add the shallots and garlic. Cook them gently for 5 minutes, until softened.

3 Add the fresh mushrooms and cook for a further 5 minutes until liquid begins to ooze from them. Add the soaked porcini, the reserved soaking liquid and the stock and bring to the boil. Reduce the heat, cover and simmer for 20 minutes.

4 Using a blender, or hand held blender, liquidise the soup until smooth. You may need to do this in batches. Return to the pan to warm through.

5 Mix the cornflour with a little cold water to make a paste and add this to the soup. Cook, stirring continuously, until the liquid thickens a little. Season to taste, stir in the parsley and ladle the soup into two warmed bowls.

Chilli and bean soup

Serves 2
266 calories per serving
Takes 25 minutes

**calorie controlled cooking
  spray**
1 leek, sliced
**250 g (9 oz) potatoes, peeled
  and diced**
1 carrot, peeled and diced
1 celery stick, chopped
2 garlic cloves, chopped
2 teaspoons chilli powder
**410 g can kidney beans,
  drained and rinsed**
**700 ml (1¼ pints) vegetable
  stock**
**2 tablespoons chopped fresh
  parsley, to garnish**

This hearty soup has a touch of chilli to warm it up.

1 Lightly spray a large, lidded, non stick saucepan with the cooking spray and heat until hot. Add the leek and stir fry for 3 minutes. Add the potatoes, carrot, celery, garlic and chilli powder. Stir fry for a further 1 minute.

2 Add the beans and stock. Bring to the boil, cover and simmer for 10 minutes until all the vegetables are tender.

3 Serve in warmed bowls, garnished with the parsley.

Variation... Any sort of canned bean will work in this soup – try butter beans.

Chunky haddock chowder

Serves 4
343 calories per serving
Takes 25 minutes
❄

**calorie controlled cooking
spray**
450 g (1 lb) leeks, sliced
**450 g (1 lb) potatoes, peeled
and cut into bite size pieces**
2 carrots, peeled and diced
**1.2 litres (2 pints) vegetable or
fish stock**
1 bouquet garni
2 bay leaves
**450 g (1 lb) undyed smoked
haddock, skinned and cut
into bite size pieces**
**6 tablespoons canned
sweetcorn, drained**
**3 tablespoons half fat crème
fraîche**
freshly ground black pepper

*This substantial main meal soup is packed with nutritious
smoked haddock and vegetables and is surprisingly filling.*

1 Spray a large, lidded, non stick saucepan with the cooking
spray. Add the leeks, potatoes and carrots and sauté for
5 minutes with the lid on, stirring occasionally.

2 Pour in the stock, add the bouquet garni and bay leaves and
bring to the boil. Reduce the heat and simmer, half covered, for
10 minutes.

3 Add the haddock and sweetcorn and cook for another
3 minutes. Remove from the heat and stir in the crème fraîche.
Remove the bouquet garni and bay leaves and season with
freshly ground black pepper before ladling into warmed serving
bowls.

Chilled and refreshing salads

Boursin, tomato and turkey salad

Serves 2
157 calories per serving
Takes 15 minutes

1 bag mixed salad leaves
2 plum tomatoes, sliced into thin wedges
75 g (2¾ oz) Boursin Light
25 g (1 oz) turkey rasher
3 tablespoons skimmed milk
1 tablespoon chopped fresh herbs (e.g. chives, parsley, basil)
freshly ground black pepper

Boursin adds a creamy garlic flavour to this simple salad.

1 Divide the mixed leaves between two serving plates. Add a sliced tomato to each.

2 Reserve about one third of the Boursin and divide the remainder between the salads, scooping it into small spoonfuls.

3 Preheat the grill to medium-high and grill the turkey rasher until crisp.

4 Meanwhile, mix the remaining Boursin with the milk and herbs to make a dressing. Season with a little black pepper.

5 Snip the turkey rasher into pieces over the salads, drizzle with the dressing and serve at once.

Variation... Use low fat soft cheese instead of Boursin, if you like, and simply use ordinary tomatoes if plum tomatoes are not available.

Chilli, crab and mango salad

Serves 4
187 calories per serving
Takes 10 minutes

2 x 170 g cans white crab
  meat, drained
1 cucumber, grated
8 radishes, sliced thinly
1 large ripe mango, peeled,
  stoned and sliced
2 teaspoons caster sugar
1½ teaspoons fish sauce
1 teaspoon dried crushed
  chillies
juice of 2 limes
1 bag mixed salad leaves
1 small red chilli, de-seeded
  and chopped finely
50 g (1¾ oz) roasted peanuts,
  chopped
2 heaped tablespoons
  chopped fresh coriander
salt

Simple but stylish, this salad has a real zing.

1 Put the crab meat in a bowl with all the other ingredients except the salad leaves, fresh chilli, peanuts, coriander and salt. Add salt to taste and toss together gently.

2 Divide the salad leaves between four serving plates and top with the crab mixture. Sprinkle the chilli, peanuts and coriander over the salad and serve.

Sweet potato and sausage salad

Serves 4

267 calories per serving

Takes 15 minutes to prepare + cooling, 30 minutes to cook

600 g (1 lb 5 oz) sweet potatoes, scrubbed and cut into wedges

calorie controlled cooking spray

4 low fat sausages (227 g/8 oz total weight)

4 shallots, chopped finely

a small bunch of fresh chives, chopped

salt and freshly ground black pepper

For the dressing

4 tablespoons half fat crème fraîche

1 tablespoon Dijon mustard

Roasted sweet potatoes are delicious eaten hot or cold and make a great salad ingredient, especially when combined with sausage and a creamy mustard dressing.

1 Preheat the oven to Gas Mark 7/220°C/fan oven 200°C. Place the sweet potatoes in a roasting tin, spray with the cooking spray, season and roast for 30 minutes until tender.

2 Meanwhile, preheat the grill to medium-high and grill the sausages for about 5 minutes on each side until browned and cooked through. Leave to cool and then chop into pieces.

3 Heat a non stick frying pan, spray with the cooking spray and stir fry the shallots for 5 minutes until softened, adding a splash of water if they start to stick.

4 Place the sweet potatoes, sausages, shallots and chives in a bowl. In a separate bowl stir together the dressing ingredients and then spoon over the potatoes. Toss the salad together and serve.

Squid salad

Serves 4
124 calories per serving
Takes 20 minutes + cooling

850 ml (1½ pints) fish stock
300 g (10½ oz) fresh squid, sliced, keeping the tentacles whole
1 cucumber, cut in half lengthways, de-seeded and sliced thinly into half moons
1 tablespoon sesame seeds
100 g (3½ oz) leaves from a Chinese leaf lettuce, chopped

For the dressing
juice of a lime
1 teaspoon fish sauce
1 tablespoon soy sauce
1 fresh red chilli, de-seeded and chopped finely
2 spring onions, sliced
1 teaspoon caster sugar
2 tablespoons chopped fresh coriander
salt and freshly ground black pepper

A fresh tasting salad bursting with flavour.

1 Whisk all the dressing ingredients together except for the coriander.

2 In a saucepan, bring the stock to a gentle simmer and add the squid. Simmer for 3–4 minutes. Drain the squid and put it into a bowl.

3 Add the coriander to the dressing and then pour it over the squid. Leave to cool.

4 Add the cucumber, sesame seeds and Chinese leaves to the bowl and mix gently.

5 Check the seasoning, adding more if necessary, and serve.

Caesar salad with smoked mackerel and Parmesan

Serves 4
551 calories per serving
Takes 10 minutes

1 Cos or Romaine lettuce
4 x 125 g (4½ oz) peppered
  smoked mackerel fillets,
  skinned
8 tablespoons low fat natural
  yogurt
1 teaspoon wholegrain or
  Dijon mustard
1 teaspoon horseradish sauce
  (optional)
28 g (1¼ oz) croûtons
20 g (¾ oz) grated Parmesan
  cheese
salt and freshly ground black
  pepper

*A twist on the traditional Caesar salad, with peppery
smoked mackerel instead of chicken.*

1 Tear the lettuce leaves roughly and divide between four
serving plates. Break up the mackerel fillets into large chunks,
removing any bones. Divide the pieces between the salads.

2 Mix together the yogurt, mustard and horseradish sauce,
if using. Season and then drizzle over the salads and toss
together.

3 Divide the croûtons evenly between each salad, scattering
over the top, followed by the Parmesan cheese.

Variation... Use smoked mackerel without the pepper, if
you like.

Smoked chicken salad

Serves 2
199 calories per serving
Takes 10 minutes

½ small Batavia or curly
  lettuce, leaves separated

100 g (3½ oz) cucumber,
  halved and sliced thinly on
  the diagonal

150 g (5½ oz) cherry
  tomatoes, halved

½ yellow pepper, de-seeded
  and sliced into rings

1 tablespoon French mustard

2 teaspoons light soy sauce

2 teaspoons runny honey

1 tablespoon white wine
  vinegar

100 g packet cooked sliced
  smoked chicken

25 g (1 oz) croûtons

salt and freshly ground black
  pepper

*If you can't find this smoked and herb-infused chicken,
then leftover roast chicken will work just as well.*

1 Put the lettuce, cucumber, tomatoes and pepper into a salad
bowl. In a jug, whisk together the mustard, soy sauce, honey
and vinegar until smooth and then season.

2 Divide the salad between two plates and top with the
chicken and croûtons. Drizzle over the dressing and serve
immediately.

Tuna and pasta salad with artichokes

Serves 4

196 calories per serving

Takes 20 minutes

100 g (3½ oz) dried small
pasta shapes

100 g (3½ oz) green beans,
trimmed and sliced

397 g can artichoke hearts in
brine, drained and halved

4 tomatoes, chopped

200 g can tuna in brine or
water, drained and flaked

1 tablespoon chopped fresh
chives or parsley

1 garlic clove, crushed

finely grated zest of a lemon

2 tablespoons lemon juice

1 tablespoon olive oil

salt and freshly ground black
pepper

*You just need to raid the store cupboard to make this easy
substantial salad in a matter of minutes.*

1 Bring a saucepan of water to the boil, add the pasta and
cook for about 8–10 minutes, or according to the packet
instructions, until just tender.

2 At the same time, bring another saucepan of water to the
boil, add the green beans and cook for about 3–4 minutes,
until cooked yet crunchy. Drain and rinse with cold water to
cool quickly.

3 Put the green beans, artichoke hearts, tomatoes, tuna and
chives or parsley into a large salad bowl and toss together.
Add the drained cooked pasta and stir well.

4 Mix together the garlic, lemon zest, lemon juice and olive
oil. Season and mix well to make the dressing. Spoon over
the salad just before serving.

Tip... This salad is excellent for packed lunches and
picnics, so just pack up a portion and take it with you.

Tabbouleh salad

Serves 4
180 calories per serving
Takes 35 minutes + 2 hours
chilling

Tabbouleh is a speciality of Lebanon. There are many versions but bulgar wheat, aromatic herbs, tomatoes and spring onions are the basic ingredients. It's traditionally served in Cos lettuce leaves, which act as bowls, but it is equally tasty straight from a lunchbox at work.

200 g (7 oz) dried bulgar wheat

½ a kettleful of boiling water

250 g (9 oz) cherry tomatoes, quartered

20 cm (8 inches) cucumber, peeled, de-seeded and diced

6 spring onions, chopped

4 tablespoons chopped fresh parsley

3 tablespoons chopped fresh mint, plus a sprig to garnish

5 tablespoons lemon juice

3 tablespoons tomato juice

1 garlic clove, crushed (optional)

salt and freshly ground black pepper

4 large lettuce leaves such as Cos or Iceberg (optional), to serve

1 Place the bulgar wheat in a large heatproof jug and pour over enough boiling water to cover it. Leave to one side for 30 minutes.

2 Meanwhile, mix the tomatoes, cucumber, spring onions and herbs together in a large salad or mixing bowl. Mix together the lemon juice, tomato juice and garlic, if using.

3 Once the bulgar wheat is ready, drain it thoroughly (see Tip) and add it to the vegetables. Add the lemon and tomato mixture and stir well. Season, but bear in mind that the flavour will develop further over the next couple of hours.

4 Cover with cling film and leave in the fridge for at least 2 hours. It will keep well if made up to 36 hours in advance. If you are using lettuce leaves to serve the tabbouleh in, put them in four shallow bowls, check the seasoning and share the tabbouleh between them. Garnish with the reserved mint sprig.

Tip... When trying to remove excess moisture from bulgar wheat (or vegetables such as cabbage or spinach), first drain in a fine mesh colander or sieve. Then, using a small bowl, push the bowl bottom side down on to the bulgar wheat. This will squeeze out any last drops of water.

Smoked trout and potato salad

Serves 2
262 calories per serving
Takes 25 minutes

350 g (12 oz) baby new
  potatoes, scrubbed and
  halved
100 g (3½ oz) low fat plain
  fromage frais
2 teaspoons wholegrain
  mustard
1 teaspoon Dijon mustard
6 cornichons (mini gherkins),
  diced finely
2 spring onions, sliced thinly
75 g (2¾ oz) baby spinach
  leaves, washed
125 g (4½ oz) smoked trout
  fillets

*The combination of smoked trout and potatoes in a creamy
mustard dressing tastes delicious. This salad can be served
slightly warm or, once it is cool, packed into a lunchbox to
take to work the next day.*

1 Bring a saucepan of water to the boil, add the potatoes and
cook for 15 minutes or until tender.

2 Meanwhile, mix the fromage frais together with the two
mustards, cornichons and spring onions to make the dressing.

3 When the potatoes are ready, drain and leave them to cool
for 5 minutes before mixing them with the dressing.

4 Divide the spinach leaves between two bowls or plates and
spoon the potatoes on top. Break up the trout fillets into chunky
flakes and scatter over the potatoes.

Tip... Cornichons are miniature pickled gherkins. They have
a lovely sweet-sharp taste and add a crunchy texture to
this salad.

Paprika Feta salad

Serves 4
107 calories per serving
Takes 15 minutes

200 g (7 oz) Feta light cheese, diced

¼ teaspoon ground cumin

½ teaspoon paprika

1 tablespoon finely chopped fresh mint

½ tablespoon finely chopped fresh dill

1 teaspoon dried herbes de Provence

juice of a lemon

2 Little Gem lettuces, shredded finely

100 g (3½ oz) red cabbage, shredded finely

2 celery sticks, sliced

3 spring onions, sliced finely

2 tablespoons fat free Italian style dressing

Perfect as a light lunch or picnic treat. Serve with a toasted medium pitta bread per person.

1 In a bowl, mix together the Feta cheese, cumin, paprika, mint, dill, herbes de Provence and lemon juice. Set aside.

2 In a large salad bowl, gently mix together the lettuces, red cabbage, celery and spring onions.

3 Add the fat free dressing to the salad and lightly toss. Scatter over the Feta mixture and serve immediately.

Mexican chicken and rice salad

Serves 4
372 calories per serving
Takes 35 minutes

175 g (6 oz) dried brown rice

125 g (4½ oz) frozen
  sweetcorn

300 g (10½ oz) skinless
  boneless chicken breasts,
  sliced into strips

juice of a lime

1 tablespoon ground cumin

½ teaspoon chilli powder

1 red pepper, de-seeded and
  diced

1 avocado, peeled, stoned and
  diced

salt and freshly ground black
  pepper

A good lunchbox salad.

1 Bring a saucepan of water to the boil, add the rice and cook
according to the packet instructions until tender, adding the
frozen sweetcorn for the last 5 minutes of the cooking time.

2 Meanwhile, toss the chicken with half the lime juice and the
cumin and chilli powder. Set aside for 5 minutes. Preheat the
grill to medium-high.

3 Grill the chicken strips for 10 minutes, turning after 5 minutes,
until cooked through. Leave to cool.

4 Drain the rice and sweetcorn, rinse in cold water and then
drain well again. Mix together with the rest of the lime juice
and the diced pepper and avocado. Season to taste. Slice the
chicken fillets across to make little chunks and serve on top
of the rice salad.

Variation... Make a vegetarian version by replacing the
chicken with 300 g (10½ oz) of Quorn Chicken Style Pieces.

Potato salad with bacon

Serves 4

226 calories per serving

Takes 5 minutes to prepare + cooling, 30 minutes to cook

800 g (1 lb 11 oz) waxy potatoes (see Tip)

a small bunch of fresh chives, chopped

1 tablespoon Dijon mustard

4 tablespoons low fat mayonnaise

2 x 25 g (1 oz) lean back bacon rashers, cut into small strips

salt and freshly ground black pepper

A classic potato salad to accompany a barbecue or to take on a picnic.

1 Bring a large saucepan of water to the boil, add the potatoes and cook for 20–30 minutes until tender. Drain and set aside to cool. Chop into cubes.

2 Add all the other ingredients, except the bacon, to the potatoes and toss together.

3 Dry fry the bacon in a non stick frying pan for 5 minutes until really crispy, scatter over the top of the salad and serve.

Tip... The potato skins can be left on or you may wish to peel them after they are cooked.

Variation... For a vegetarian version, just omit the bacon.

Chinese prawn and noodle salad

Serves 4
242 calories per serving
Takes 10 minutes

125 g (4½ oz) dried medium
 egg noodles
220 g can pineapple slices in
 natural juice, diced and juice
 reserved
2 tablespoons soy sauce
1 teaspoon grated fresh root
 ginger
½ red pepper, de-seeded and
 sliced thinly
½ yellow pepper, de-seeded
 and sliced thinly
½ green pepper, de-seeded
 and sliced thinly
175 g (6 oz) beansprouts
250 g (9 oz) cooked peeled
 prawns, defrosted if frozen

A superb salad for a working lunch.

1 Bring a saucepan of water to the boil, add the noodles and
cook for 5 minutes, or according to the packet instructions,
until tender.

2 Meanwhile, measure 4 tablespoons of juice from the
pineapple can into a large bowl and stir in the soy sauce and
grated ginger. Add the pineapple to the bowl along with the
peppers and beansprouts.

3 Drain the noodles and refresh in cold water. Snip into slightly
shorter lengths using kitchen scissors and then mix the noodles
and prawns into the pineapple and vegetables. Serve in bowls
or take to work in a sealed container.

Tikka chicken salad

Serves 4
237 calories per serving
Takes 10 minutes

450 g (1 lb) cooked chicken tikka pieces
225 g (8 oz) tomatoes, de-seeded and chopped
6 spring onions, sliced
2 green chillies, de-seeded and chopped finely
2 tablespoons chopped fresh coriander
salt and freshly ground black pepper
salad leaves, to serve

For the dressing
150 g (5½ oz) 0% fat Greek style yogurt
juice of a lime
1 tablespoon chopped fresh parsley
1 tablespoon chopped fresh chives
1 tablespoon chopped fresh mint
½ teaspoon Dijon mustard
freshly ground black pepper

This quick salad makes use of ready flavoured chicken breasts.

1 Mix all the dressing ingredients together in a jug.

2 In a large bowl, toss the chicken with the tomatoes, spring onions, chillies and coriander.

3 Toss the chicken mixture with the dressing and check the seasoning.

4 Arrange the salad leaves on plates and spoon the chicken on top.

Chilli bean salad

Serves 2
215 calories per serving
Takes 20 minutes

2 x 25 g (1 oz) lean back
  bacon rashers
200 g can kidney beans,
  drained and rinsed
1 celery stick, sliced thinly
2 spring onions, chopped
1 carrot, peeled and grated
  coarsely
1 tomato, chopped
2 tablespoons fat free French
  dressing
a few drops of Tabasco sauce
4–6 large lettuce leaves
40 g (1½ oz) half fat Cheddar,
  cubed
1 punnet mustard cress
salt and freshly ground black
  pepper

Kidney beans can form a great basis for a fast and filling salad or light meal. This delicious salad tastes superb served with 1 rye crispbread per person.

1 Preheat the grill to medium-high and grill the bacon rashers for about 3–4 minutes until they are crispy. Cool and then chop them finely. Set aside.

2 Place the kidney beans in a large mixing bowl. Stir in the celery, spring onions, carrot and tomato. Add the dressing, Tabasco sauce and chopped bacon and season.

3 Line two shallow bowls with the lettuce leaves and divide the bean salad between the bowls.

4 Scatter the cheese and mustard cress over the salad. Serve it immediately or lightly chill it in the fridge until you are ready to eat.

Variation... Try using a 170 g can of sweetcorn and 100 g (3½ oz) of whole green beans, blanched, instead of the kidney beans.

Smoked mackerel and beetroot salad

Serves 4

271 calories per serving

Takes 10 minutes to prepare
+ 30 minutes soaking

In this recipe, salty smoked mackerel is complemented by sweet beetroot and nutty bulgar wheat to make a salad full of interesting flavours and textures, served with a creamy mustard dressing.

100 g (3½ oz) dried bulgar wheat

300 ml (10 fl oz) boiling water

8 small cooked beetroot, diced finely

150 g (5½ oz) peppered smoked mackerel fillet, skinned and flaked

a small bunch of fresh chives, chopped, plus extra to garnish

juice of ½ a lemon

2 tablespoons half fat crème fraîche

2 teaspoons wholegrain mustard

225 g (8 oz) rocket or mixed baby salad leaves

1 Place the bulgar wheat in a bowl, pour over the boiling water and leave to soak for 30 minutes.

2 Meanwhile, place the beetroot, mackerel flakes and chopped chives in a large bowl. Squeeze the lemon juice over and add the crème fraîche and mustard.

3 Arrange the salad leaves in nests on four serving plates. When the bulgar wheat is swollen, drain and rinse in cold water. Drain again thoroughly. Add to the beetroot mixture in the bowl and very gently mix together.

4 Pile spoonfuls of the salad on top of the salad leaves, sprinkle with the extra chives and serve.

Salade Niçoise

Serves 4
258 calories per serving
Takes 20 minutes to prepare,
    15 minutes to cook

450 g (1 lb) new potatoes,
    scrubbed and halved if large
a fresh mint sprig
4 eggs
200 g (7 oz) green beans,
    trimmed
200 g can tuna in brine,
    drained
225 g (8 oz) cherry tomatoes,
    halved
1 small red onion, sliced thinly
12 black olives, stoned
a bunch of fresh basil,
    chopped roughly
2 Little Gem lettuces, leaves
    separated

For the vinaigrette
grated zest and juice of a
    lemon
1 teaspoon wholegrain
    mustard
2 tablespoons virtually fat free
    fromage frais
salt and freshly ground black
    pepper

*An authentic version of this famous salad from Nice in the
south of France.*

1 Bring two saucepans of water to the boil. Add the potatoes
and mint to one saucepan and cook for 10–15 minutes or until
just tender. Add the eggs to the second saucepan and cook for
10 minutes. Steam the green beans over one of the pans until
just cooked, about 2–4 minutes.

2 Drain the eggs and immediately put them under a cold tap
to cool them rapidly. Peel, slice them into quarters and put
them in a large bowl with all the other ingredients for the salad,
including the green beans. When the potatoes are cooked,
drain and add them to the bowl.

3 Whisk together all the vinaigrette ingredients and then pour
the vinaigrette over the salad. Toss everything together very
gently. Check the seasoning and serve.

Tip... Putting the eggs into boiling water and then cooling
them rapidly under the cold tap ensures that the yolks stay
a lovely yellow colour.

Variation... Other ingredients to try are capers, red peppers,
fresh tuna, anchovies and flat leaf parsley.

Mango, watercress and Wensleydale salad

Serves 4
181 calories per serving
Takes 10 minutes to prepare
Ⓥ

1 bag mixed salad leaves
a bunch of watercress
fresh herb sprigs (e.g. marjoram, thyme or mint)
125 g (4½ oz) red or green seedless grapes, halved
1 large ripe mango
125 g (4½ oz) Wensleydale cheese
4 tablespoons fat free mustard and honey or vinaigrette style dressing
salt and freshly ground black pepper

Mango is a wonderful fruit and it's delicious in this refreshing salad where it perfectly complements the flavour of mild honey-tasting Wensleydale cheese.

1 Arrange the salad leaves and watercress on four serving plates and scatter with a few fresh herbs. Sprinkle with the grapes.

2 To prepare the mango, slice around the large flat stone and then peel and chop the flesh. Scatter over the salads.

3 Crumble the cheese and divide equally between the plates. Drizzle a tablespoon of the dressing over each portion and sprinkle with a little seasoning. Garnish with a few extra herbs and serve at once.

Tip... Choose a ripe mango – it should 'give' a little when pressed gently with your thumb.

Variations... Try using Lancashire cheese or a white Cheshire instead of Wensleydale – either will be excellent in this salad.

If you like, use papaya instead of mango.

Avocado and crab salad

Serves 2
249 calories per serving
Takes 10 minutes

170 g can crab meat, drained
½ large mango, peeled, stoned
    and chopped
½ teaspoon finely diced red
    chilli
grated zest and juice of a lime
a good handful of chopped
    Iceberg lettuce leaves
1 small avocado, peeled,
    stoned and sliced
8 cherry tomatoes
salt and freshly ground black
    pepper

The lime and chilli give this salad a delicious Thai flavour.

1 Mix together the crab meat, mango, chilli, lime zest and half the lime juice. Season.

2 Divide the lettuce between two plates and spoon the crab mixture on top. Serve with the avocado slices, cherry tomatoes and the remaining lime juice drizzled over.

Variation... Try this mixture with a 200 g can of drained tuna in brine or water instead of the crab meat.

Minestrone salad

Serves 2
178 calories per serving
Takes 15 minutes

75 g (2¾ oz) dried wholewheat
spaghetti, broken into short
lengths

60 g (2 oz) fine green beans,
trimmed and halved

30 g (1¼ oz) frozen peas

2 baby courgettes, sliced

½ fennel bulb, sliced finely

½ teaspoon vegetable gravy
granules

1 teaspoon Dijon mustard

75 g (2¾ oz) red or yellow
cherry tomatoes, halved

a generous handful of fresh
basil leaves

a generous handful of fresh
parsley leaves

salt and freshly ground black
pepper

*All the flavours of the traditional soup but in a salad.
Delightfully different.*

1 Bring a large saucepan of water to the boil, add the
pasta and cook for 5–6 minutes or according to the packet
instructions. Add the beans, peas, courgettes and fennel and
cook for 2–3 minutes until just tender. Drain, reserving a
ladleful of cooking liquid (about 50 ml/2 fl oz). Rinse the
pasta and vegetables in cold water until cold. Drain again
thoroughly and put into a salad bowl.

2 Mix the gravy granules and mustard into the hot reserved
cooking liquid until slightly thickened. Add this and the
tomatoes, basil and parsley leaves to the salad bowl. Toss
to combine. Check the seasoning and serve immediately.

Variation... You can add 100 g (3½ oz) of torn wafer thin
ham to the salad bowl.

Fresh salmon salad

Serves 2
264 calories per serving
Takes 5 minutes

1 small courgette, grated
1 avocado, peeled, stoned and
  cut into thick slices
grated zest and juice of a
  small lemon
75 g (2¾ oz) low fat fromage
  frais
1 teaspoon mint sauce
75 g (2¾ oz) cucumber,
  de-seeded and diced finely
50 g (1¾ oz) pea shoots
100 g (3½ oz) smoked salmon
freshly ground black pepper

Pea shoots are young, tender tips of garden peas that have a distinctive 'pea' flavour, making them the perfect salad leaf. But if you can't find them, lamb's lettuce is a great alternative.

1 Mix together the courgette, avocado, lemon zest and lemon juice in a bowl and season with freshly ground black pepper. Set aside.

2 In a small bowl, mix together the fromage frais, mint sauce and cucumber. Season with freshly ground black pepper.

3 Divide the pea shoots between two plates and scatter over the courgette and avocado mixture. Top with folds of smoked salmon and a generous dollop of the cucumber mixture. Serve immediately.

Warm and surprising salads

Roasted tomato and mozzarella salad

Serves 2
141 calories per serving
Takes 25 minutes

calorie controlled cooking
spray
5 large plum tomatoes, halved
2 teaspoons balsamic vinegar
**125 g (4½ oz) mozzarella light,
drained and torn**
**salt and freshly ground black
pepper**
fresh basil leaves, to garnish

For the dressing
1 tablespoon low fat pesto
a squeeze of fresh lemon juice

A variation on the classic summer salad.

1 Preheat the oven to Gas Mark 6/200°C/fan oven 180°C.
Spray a baking tray with the cooking spray.

2 Toss the tomatoes in the balsamic vinegar and place, cut
side down, on the baking tray. Spray again with the cooking
spray. Roast the tomatoes for 15 minutes until they are
softened but still retain their shape and are slightly blackened
on the edges.

3 Meanwhile, make the dressing by mixing together the pesto,
lemon juice and 1½ tablespoons of water.

4 Place the roasted tomatoes on two serving plates and top
with the torn mozzarella. Drizzle over the pesto dressing,
season and scatter over the basil leaves.

Lentil and herb salad

Serves 4

97 calories per serving

Takes 15 minutes to prepare,
25 minutes to cook

100 g (3½ oz) dried Puy lentils
1 teaspoon olive oil
1 large red onion, diced
1 garlic clove, sliced
1 courgette, sliced thinly
1 tablespoon balsamic vinegar
a large bunch of fresh mint,
    chopped
100 g (3½ oz) baby spinach,
    washed
salt and freshly ground black
    pepper

*A healthy but also a very filling and tasty salad – eat it on
its own or with your favourite fish dish.*

1 Bring a medium saucepan of water to the boil, add the lentils
and simmer for 15 minutes until the lentils are cooked but still
firm. Keep checking that the water doesn't boil dry and add a
little more if necessary.

2 Meanwhile, heat the olive oil in a non stick frying pan and
add the red onion and garlic. Cook gently, stirring occasionally,
until they start to soften.

3 Add the courgette and continue to cook, stirring occasionally,
for 6–8 minutes.

4 When the lentils are cooked, drain thoroughly and then add
them to the frying pan with the balsamic vinegar. Stir well and
season. Remove the pan from the heat and add the mint. Leave
the mixture to cool slightly.

5 Place the spinach in a shallow serving dish or platter and
spoon the lentil mixture over the top to serve.

Variation... For a slightly spicy meaty version, see the
recipe on page 142.

Marinated chicken salad

Serves 4
288 calories per serving
Takes 10 minutes to prepare
+ 20 minutes marinating,
40 minutes to cook

4 x 125 g (4½ oz) skinless
boneless chicken breasts

1 tablespoon chopped fresh
rosemary

finely grated zest and juice
of 2 limes, plus wedges to
serve

2 garlic cloves, sliced

1 red chilli, de-seeded and
diced

1 large courgette, cut into
chunks

450 g (1 lb) sweet potato,
peeled and cut into chunks

2 red peppers, de-seeded and
cut into chunks

calorie controlled cooking
spray

salt and freshly ground black
pepper

To serve
mixed salad leaves
fat free vinaigrette

A touch of chilli adds a little spice to this delicious
Mediterranean style salad.

1 Place the chicken breasts, rosemary, lime zest and juice,
garlic and chilli in a large non metallic bowl. Stir well to coat
the meat. Cover and leave to marinate at room temperature
for 20 minutes.

2 Meanwhile, preheat the oven to Gas Mark 6/200°C/fan oven
180°C. Place the vegetables in a large roasting tin, spray with
the cooking spray and roast for 20 minutes.

3 Remove from the oven, add the chicken breasts and any
marinade on top of the vegetables and season. Spray again
with the cooking spray. Roast for a further 20 minutes until
the chicken is cooked – a skewer inserted into the thickest
part of the chicken should make the juices run clear.

4 Slice each chicken breast and serve on top of a quarter
of the vegetables with some salad leaves and vinaigrette
drizzled over.

Ⓥ **Variation...** For a fantastic vegetarian version, see the
recipe on page 157.

Sicilian steak salad

Serves 4

220 calories per serving

Takes 20 minutes +
20 minutes marinating

2 small fresh rosemary sprigs,
needles only

1 tablespoon roughly chopped
fresh parsley

juice of ½ a lemon

400 g (14 oz) sirloin steak,
trimmed of visible fat

25 g (1 oz) pine nut kernels

25 g (1 oz) raisins

75 ml (3 fl oz) balsamic
vinegar

85 g bag watercress

1 Little Gem lettuce, shredded

8 cherry tomatoes, halved

salt and freshly ground black
pepper

*Fresh herbs, raisins and nuts give this unusual salad its
Sicilian flavours.*

1 Roughly crush the rosemary in a pestle and mortar, mixing
in the parsley and lemon juice. Season the steak on both sides
and then smear the rough paste over the meat. Cover and set
aside to marinate for 20 minutes.

2 Meanwhile, toast the pine nut kernels in a small non stick
frying pan over a medium heat, stirring regularly for a minute
or so until they are golden. Remove from the pan and set aside.

3 Heat the same frying pan until hot, add the steak and cook
for 2–3 minutes, turning once. If you like your steak well done,
cook for 5–6 minutes. Remove from the pan to a plate and
cover with foil to rest and keep warm.

4 Return the pan to the heat. Add the raisins and the balsamic
vinegar, which will sizzle. Swirl to deglaze the pan and loosen
any meat bits, reduce the heat and simmer for a minute or two
until slightly syrupy.

5 To serve, divide the watercress, lettuce and tomatoes
between four plates. Slice the steak and place on top. Scatter
over the pine nut kernels and drizzle over the balsamic raisins.

Variation... You can replace the pine nut kernels with the
same quantity of sunflower seeds.

Warm goat's cheese salad

Serves 2
136 calories per serving
Takes 15 minutes

½ pomegranate
2 teaspoons white or regular balsamic vinegar
a pinch of artificial sweetener
2 x 40 g (1½ oz) slices medium fat goat's cheese with rind
4 cm (1½ inches) cucumber, diced
6 Little Gem lettuce leaves, shredded
4 cherry tomatoes, halved
a handful of rocket

Lightly grilled creamy goat's cheese goes exceptionally well with the slightly sweet and sour taste of pomegranate.

1 Remove around 20 seeds from the pomegranate and reserve. Press the remaining seeds still inside the shell over a lemon squeezer to extract the juice (see Tip). Sieve to remove any bits. Mix the juice with the vinegar and sweetener.

2 Preheat the grill to medium. Place the goat's cheese slices on a piece of foil and grill for 3–4 minutes until softened.

3 Arrange the cucumber, lettuce, tomatoes and rocket on two serving plates and top each with a slice of goat's cheese. Scatter over the reserved pomegranate seeds and drizzle with the dressing. Serve at once.

Tips... If you don't have a lemon squeezer, remove the red or pink pomegranate flesh and press the seeds through a metal sieve using the end of a rolling pin. Be careful, though, since they do squirt.

This can be made into a main course salad by increasing the goat's cheese to 100 g (3½ oz) per person and increasing the amount of leaves and tomatoes as required.

The salad will taste the same with regular balsamic vinegar but it discolours the cheese. White balsamic makes the salad look better when entertaining.

Chorizo and lentil salad

Serves 4

155 calories per serving

Takes 15 minutes to prepare,
25 minutes to cook

100 g (3½ oz) dried Puy lentils
1 teaspoon olive oil
1 large red onion, diced
1 garlic clove, sliced
100 g (3½ oz) chorizo sausage,
chopped
1 courgette, sliced thinly
1 tablespoon balsamic vinegar
a large bunch of fresh mint,
chopped
100 g (3½ oz) baby spinach,
washed
salt and freshly ground black
pepper

This is a tasty meaty version of the recipe on page 135.

1 Place the lentils in a medium saucepan with about 200 ml (7 fl oz) of water and bring to the boil. Simmer for 15 minutes until the lentils are cooked but still firm. Keep checking that the water doesn't boil dry and add a little more if necessary.

2 Meanwhile, heat the olive oil in a non stick frying pan and add the red onion, garlic and chorizo. Cook gently, stirring occasionally, until the onion and garlic start to soften.

3 Add the courgette and continue to cook, stirring occasionally, for 6–8 minutes.

4 When the lentils are cooked, add them to the frying pan with the balsamic vinegar. Stir well and season. Remove the pan from the heat and add the mint. Leave the mixture to cool slightly.

5 Place the spinach in a shallow serving dish or platter and spoon the lentil mixture over the top to serve.

Glazed turkey salad

Serves 4

208 calories per serving

Takes 15 minutes to prepare,
15 minutes to cook

350 g (12 oz) turkey
escalopes, cut into strips

2 tablespoons dark soy sauce

1 tablespoon tomato purée

1 garlic clove, crushed

2 teaspoons clear honey

2 teaspoons sunflower oil

150 g (5½ oz) mange tout,
halved lengthways

150 g (5½ oz) carrots, peeled
and cut into matchsticks

100 g (3½ oz) canned water
chestnuts, drained and
sliced

100 g (3½ oz) mushrooms,
sliced

6 spring onions, sliced very
finely

1 Chinese leaf lettuce,
shredded

A delicious warm salad.

1 Mix the turkey with the soy sauce, tomato purée, garlic and honey.

2 Heat the sunflower oil in a wok or large non stick frying pan. Add the turkey and stir fry for 8–10 minutes, until cooked through and a glaze starts to form a sticky coating around the strips.

3 Add the mange tout, carrots, water chestnuts and mushrooms and cook for a further 2 minutes.

4 Remove the pan from the heat and toss in the spring onions and shredded Chinese leaf lettuce. Divide between four plates and serve at once.

Tip... Turkey absorbs other flavours very well. If time permits, allow the turkey to marinate for 20 minutes so the flavours really have time to develop.

ⓥ **Variation...** For a tangy tofu vegetarian version, see the recipe on page 165.

Roasted pumpkin and pasta salad

Serves 4

225 calories per serving

Takes 25 minutes to prepare,
40 minutes to cook

1 kg (2 lb 4 oz) pumpkin or
butternut squash, peeled,
de-seeded and cut into bite
size pieces

2 carrots, peeled and cut into
chunky batons

2 red onions, cut into wedges

1 orange pepper, de-seeded
and cut into strips

16 cherry tomatoes, halved

2 fresh rosemary sprigs

calorie controlled cooking
spray

150 g (5½ oz) dried pasta
shapes (e.g. fusilli)

4 tablespoons balsamic
vinegar

salt and freshly ground black
pepper

*Roasted vegetables give this colourful salad lots of lovely
flavour, and the balsamic vinegar adds a delicious tang.*

1 Preheat the oven to Gas Mark 6/200°C/fan oven 180°C.

2 Place all the vegetables and the rosemary in a large roasting
tin and spray with the cooking spray. Roast in the oven for
40 minutes until tender and beginning to char. You will need
to turn them occasionally.

3 Meanwhile, bring a saucepan of water to the boil, add the
pasta and cook according to the packet instructions. Drain and
rinse in cold water.

4 Mix the vegetables into the pasta, season and drizzle over
the balsamic vinegar. Allow to cool a little before serving.

Variation... You could add 4 Quorn Deli Bacon Style
Rashers, grilled until cooked and then chopped.

Breakfast salad

Serves 4

206 calories per serving

Takes 15 minutes to prepare,
15 minutes to cook

225 g (8 oz) low fat sausages
150 g (5½ oz) lean back bacon
calorie controlled cooking
spray
225 g (8 oz) open cup
mushrooms, sliced
225 g (8 oz) cherry tomatoes,
halved
1 tablespoon wholegrain
mustard
1 tablespoon dark soy sauce
1 teaspoon clear honey
350 g (12 oz) Iceberg lettuce,
shredded

*This substantial salad is perfect for a lunchtime treat or
brunch to stave off those hunger pangs.*

1 Preheat the grill to medium-high and grill the sausages for
about 10 minutes until evenly browned and cooked through.
Grill the bacon until crispy. Slice the sausages into rings and
chop the bacon into small pieces.

2 Meanwhile, spray a non stick frying pan with the cooking
spray and add the mushrooms. Cook them for 5 minutes until
they are tender.

3 Add the tomatoes, mustard, soy sauce and honey and cook
for a further 2 minutes, stirring occasionally. Add the sausages
and bacon and mix everything well.

4 Divide the Iceberg lettuce between four serving plates and
top with the 'breakfast' mix. Serve at once.

☉ Variation... For a vegetarian alternative, omit the bacon
and use vegetarian sausages instead.

Chicken and couscous salad

Serves 2

364 calories per serving

Takes 30 minutes

❄

**2 courgettes, halved and
  sliced thinly lengthways**

**1 red pepper, de-seeded and
  cut into wedges**

**150 g (5½ oz) skinless
  boneless chicken breast,
  thinly sliced**

**calorie controlled cooking
  spray**

100 g (3½ oz) dried couscous

½ a kettleful of boiling water

**100 g (3½ oz) cherry
  tomatoes, halved**

**grated zest and juice of ½ a
  lemon**

**salt and freshly ground black
  pepper**

For the minted yogurt dressing

**150 g (5½ oz) low fat natural
  yogurt**

juice of ½ a small lemon

**a small bunch of fresh mint,
  chopped finely**

**salt and freshly ground black
  pepper**

*This substantial salad is served with a delicious minted
yogurt dressing that can be used to liven up any salad
vegetables or steamed greens.*

1 Line a grill pan with foil and spread the courgettes, pepper
and chicken strips out over it. (You may have to do this in two
or three batches depending on the size of your grill pan.)

2 Spray with the cooking spray, season and then grill for
3–4 minutes. Turn over and grill for a further 3–4 minutes
until the chicken is cooked through and golden.

3 Place the couscous in a large bowl and cover with boiling
water. Cover with a lid or plate and leave to steam for
10 minutes, then fluff up with a fork.

4 Add the grilled vegetables and chicken, tomatoes, lemon
zest and juice and seasoning to the couscous and toss
together.

5 Mix the dressing ingredients together, drizzle over the salad
and serve.

Thai beef salad

Serves 1
256 calories per serving
Takes 15 minutes

125 g (4½ oz) **beef medallion or lean fillet steak**, at room temperature

calorie controlled cooking spray

1 tablespoon **fish sauce or soy sauce**

juice of ½ a **lime**

1 teaspoon **grated fresh root ginger**

4 cm (1½ inches) **cucumber**, cut into matchsticks

50 g (1¾ oz) **beansprouts**

60 g (2 oz) **seedless red grapes**, halved

½ **red chilli**, de-seeded and sliced

1 tablespoon **fresh mint leaves**

30 g (1¼ oz) **herb salad**

Traditionally a Thai starter, this main meal salad is a wonderful combination of sweet and sharp flavours.

1 Preheat a griddle pan or non stick frying pan on a high setting. Lightly spray the steak with the cooking spray and add to the pan. Cook it for 2 minutes on each side for rare or 3 minutes each side for medium rare. Remove the cooked steak to a plate and rest for 5 minutes before slicing thinly.

2 Meanwhile, mix the fish or soy sauce with the lime juice in a salad bowl. Squeeze the grated ginger over the bowl to extract the juice and then discard the pulp. Toss the cucumber and beansprouts in the dressing. Add the grapes, chilli, mint leaves and herb salad and mix thoroughly.

3 Arrange the steak on top of the salad, pouring any juices from the plate over the top. Serve immediately.

Tip... For the best results, the steak should be cooked rare to medium rare in this recipe in order to keep the meat succulent and juicy.

Warm broccoli and cheese salad

Serves 2
245 calories per serving
Takes 20 minutes

¼ kettleful of boiling water

1 head of broccoli, cut into even sized florets

calorie controlled cooking spray

1 garlic clove, crushed

4 spring onions or 1 shallot, sliced finely

1 tablespoon pine nut kernels

1 tablespoon balsamic vinegar

4 cherry tomatoes, halved

50 g (1¾ oz) blue cheese, crumbled

1 tablespoon reduced fat houmous

grated zest and juice of ½ a lemon

a pinch of dried chilli flakes or a small fresh chilli, de-seeded and chopped finely (optional)

This is a stunning variation of the recipe on page 156.

1 Pour an inch of boiling water into a saucepan with a tight fitting lid. Add the broccoli, put the lid on and steam for 4–5 minutes or until just tender but still bright green. Take off the heat and set aside without draining.

2 Meanwhile, spray a large non stick saucepan with the cooking spray and stir fry the garlic, spring onions or shallot and pine nut kernels over a high heat until golden brown.

3 Add the balsamic vinegar, stir fry for a few more seconds and then reduce the heat and add the broccoli, any cooking water left in the saucepan and the tomatoes and cheese.

4 In a small bowl, mix together the houmous with the lemon zest and juice, chilli, if using, and 4 tablespoons of water to make a dressing. Pour this over the broccoli mixture, toss to coat well and then serve.

Hot bacon and plum salad

Serves 2
390 calories per serving
Takes 20 minutes

12 plums, 6 stoned and
quartered and the others left
whole
2 x 25 g (1 oz) lean back
bacon rashers
1 garlic clove, crushed
1 small green chilli,
de-seeded and chopped
finely
2 teaspoons olive oil
2 teaspoons balsamic vinegar
1 teaspoon soy sauce
1 teaspoon lime juice
a few crisp salad leaves
100 g (3½ oz) Feta cheese,
cubed
200 g (7 oz) mange tout
salt and freshly ground black
pepper

This is scrumptious and so easy to make.

1 Put the 6 whole plums in a saucepan with 4 tablespoons of water and cook for about 10 minutes, until softened.

2 Meanwhile, preheat the grill to medium-high, grill the bacon and then cut into small pieces.

3 Put the garlic, chilli, olive oil, balsamic vinegar, soy sauce, lime juice and seasoning in a small bowl and whisk together to make the dressing.

4 Push the cooked plums through a sieve. Mix this plum purée into the dressing, stirring well.

5 Arrange the salad leaves on two serving plates and then pile the Feta cheese, mange tout, quartered plums and bacon on top. Pour over the dressing and serve.

Tip... This is a great salad to make when plums are in season and plentiful. If you have more plums than you need you can cook and sieve them and then keep the purée frozen in ice cube trays.

Warm broccoli and bacon salad

Serves 2
211 calories per serving
Takes 20 minutes

¼ kettleful of boiling water
1 head of broccoli, cut into even sized florets
calorie controlled cooking spray
1 garlic clove, crushed
4 spring onions or 1 shallot, sliced finely
4 x 25 g (1 oz) lean back bacon rashers, chopped into strips
1 tablespoon pine nut kernels
1 tablespoon balsamic vinegar
4 cherry tomatoes, halved
1 tablespoon reduced fat houmous
grated zest and juice of ½ a lemon
a pinch of dried chilli flakes or a small fresh chilli, de-seeded and chopped finely (optional)

A colourful warm salad for autumn days.

1 Pour an inch of boiling water into a saucepan with a tight fitting lid. Add the broccoli, put the lid on and steam for 4–5 minutes or until just tender but still bright green. Take off the heat and set aside without draining.

2 Meanwhile, spray a large saucepan with the cooking spray and stir fry the garlic, spring onions or shallot, bacon and pine nut kernels over a high heat until golden brown.

3 Add the balsamic vinegar, stir fry for a few more seconds and then reduce the heat and add the broccoli, any cooking water left in the saucepan and the tomatoes.

4 In a small bowl, mix together the houmous with the lemon zest and juice, chilli, if using, and 4 tablespoons of water to make a dressing. Pour this over the broccoli mixture, toss to coat well and then serve.

Ⓥ Variation... For a cheesy vegetarian version, see the recipe on page 153.

Marinated vegetable salad

Serves 4

311 calories per serving

Takes 10 minutes to prepare
+ 20 minutes marinating,
40 minutes to cook

1 large courgette, cut into
   chunks

450 g (1 lb) sweet potato,
   peeled and cut into chunks

2 red peppers, de-seeded and
   cut into chunks

1 tablespoon chopped fresh
   rosemary

finely grated zest and juice
   of 2 limes, plus wedges to
   serve

2 garlic cloves, sliced

1 red chilli, de-seeded and
   diced

calorie controlled cooking
   spray

240 g (8½ oz) light halloumi
   cheese, sliced

salt and freshly ground black
   pepper

To serve

mixed salad leaves

fat free vinaigrette

*This is a tasty vegetarian version of the recipe on
page 136.*

1 Place the vegetables, rosemary, lime zest and juice, garlic,
chilli and seasoning in a large non metallic bowl. Stir well
to coat the vegetables. Cover and leave to marinate at room
temperature for 20 minutes.

2 Meanwhile, preheat the oven to Gas Mark 6/200°C/fan oven
180°C.

3 Place the vegetables in a large roasting tin, spray with the
cooking spray and roast for 40 minutes, turning once halfway
through and spraying again with the cooking spray.

4 Meanwhile, spray a large non stick frying pan with the
cooking spray and fry the halloumi slices for 2–3 minutes on
each side until golden. You may need to do this in batches.

5 Divide the roasted vegetables between four plates and top
each with a quarter of the halloumi and some salad leaves.
Drizzle over a little vinaigrette.

Zingy duck salad

Serves 2
283 calories per serving
Takes 20 minutes

300 g (10½ oz) skinless
    boneless duck breasts, cut
    into small cubes
½ teaspoon coriander seeds,
    crushed
½ teaspoon Thai 7 spice
1 tablespoon teriyaki sauce
calorie controlled cooking
    spray
½ x 150 g bag bistro salad
    leaves
100 g (3½ oz) cucumber, diced
1 large red chilli, de-seeded
    and sliced finely
½ pomegranate, seeds
    removed and reserved
grated zest of a lime
2 tablespoons 0% fat Greek
    yogurt

*Tender chunks of duck coated in coriander, Thai 7 spice
and teriyaki top this fruity salad. Delicious hot or cold.*

1 Mix together the duck, coriander seeds, Thai 7 spice and
teriyaki sauce in a bowl. Heat a non stick frying pan and spray
with the cooking spray. Cook the duck for 5–10 minutes until
cooked to your liking, turning occasionally. Transfer to a plate,
cover loosely with foil and set aside.

2 Divide the salad leaves between two plates and scatter over
the cucumber, chilli and pomegranate seeds. Mix together the
lime zest and Greek yoghurt.

3 Top each salad with half the duck cubes and a dollop of
yogurt. Serve immediately.

Tip... To remove the seeds from a pomegranate, firmly roll
the fruit between your hands, cut it in half and empty the
seeds into a bowl.

Hot peppered chicken and spinach salad

Serves 2

225 calories per serving

Takes 15 minutes to prepare,
20 minutes to cook

2 x 125 g (4½ oz) skinless boneless chicken breasts

1 tablespoon freshly ground mixed pepper

calorie controlled cooking spray

1 red skinned dessert apple (e.g. Braeburn), cored and sliced thinly

1 tablespoon fresh lemon juice

175 g (6 oz) baby spinach leaves, washed

3 tablespoons low fat natural yogurt

1 tablespoon finely chopped fresh chives

The contrasting colours of the red skinned apples and the deep green spinach make this a very attractive and appetising dish.

1 Preheat the oven to Gas Mark 6/200°C/fan oven 180°C. Line a baking tray with non stick baking parchment.

2 Season the chicken breasts generously with the mixed pepper and spray them lightly with the cooking spray. Place the chicken on the prepared baking tray and roast for 20 minutes.

3 Toss the apple slices with the lemon juice and baby spinach leaves and divide the mixture between two plates.

4 Mix the yogurt with the chives. Slice each chicken breast on the slant – each breast should give 5–6 slices. Pile the slices randomly on top of the spinach and apple. Drizzle with the yogurt and chive dressing and serve.

Tip... Add the chicken while it is still warm – this way it begins to just wilt the spinach.

Asparagus, Parma ham and nectarine salad

Serves 6
156 calories per serving
Takes 15 minutes

225 g (8 oz) asparagus tips
150 g (5½ oz) mixed baby salad leaves
6 slices Parma ham, roughly torn
20 g (¾ oz) Parmesan cheese shavings
calorie controlled cooking spray
6 ripe nectarines, stoned and sliced into wedges

For the dressing
3 tablespoons balsamic vinegar
3 tablespoons clear honey
1½ teaspoons wholegrain mustard
salt and freshly ground black pepper

Pan frying the nectarines adds an extra dimension to this salad but, if it's easier, you can just leave them raw.

1 Bring a saucepan of water to the boil, add the asparagus tips and cook for 3 minutes or until just tender. Drain and refresh in cold water to stop the cooking process.

2 Arrange the salad leaves on a large platter or shallow serving dish and top with the asparagus, Parma ham and Parmesan shavings. Whisk the dressing ingredients together and set aside.

3 When ready to serve, lightly spray a non stick frying pan with the cooking spray, add the nectarine wedges and fry for about 2 minutes until lightly caramelised; you will need to cook these in two batches. Scatter over the salad and drizzle on the dressing just before serving.

Glazed tofu salad

Serves 4

208 calories per serving

Takes 15 minutes to prepare, 15 minutes to cook

350 g (12 oz) firm tofu, cubed

2 tablespoons dark soy sauce

1 tablespoon tomato purée

1 garlic clove, crushed

2 teaspoons clear honey

2 teaspoons sunflower oil

150 g (5½ oz) mange tout, halved lengthways

150 g (5½ oz) carrots, peeled and cut into matchsticks

100 g (3½ oz) canned water chestnuts, drained and sliced

100 g (3½ oz) mushrooms, sliced

6 spring onions, sliced very finely

1 Chinese leaf lettuce, shredded

This tangy tofu salad is a great vegetarian version of the recipe on page 143.

1 Mix the tofu with the soy sauce, tomato purée, garlic and honey.

2 Heat the sunflower oil in a wok or large non stick frying pan. Stir fry the tofu for 8–10 minutes until cooked through and a glaze starts to form a sticky coating around the strips.

3 Add the mange tout, carrots, water chestnuts and mushrooms and cook for a further 2 minutes.

4 Remove the pan from the heat and toss in the spring onions and shredded Chinese leaf lettuce. Divide between four plates and serve at once.

Aubergine, spring onion and spinach salad

Serves 4
83 calories per serving
Takes 25 minutes

2 small aubergines
2 red peppers, de-seeded and cut into bite size pieces
4 tablespoons light soy sauce
4 teaspoons finely grated ginger
2 teaspoons finely chopped red chilli
1 teaspoon artificial sweetener
a bunch of spring onions, cut into long thin strips
4 handfuls of spinach leaves, washed
2 tablespoons chopped fresh coriander, to garnish

This is a warm salad with an Asian style dressing. Serve with 150 g (5½ oz) of dried wholewheat pasta, cooked according to the packet instructions.

1 Trim the ends from the aubergines and then cut long thin slices down the length. A vegetable peeler is good for this. Cut each slice in half across its width.

2 Heat a ridged griddle pan or non stick frying pan until hot. Place the aubergine slices and pepper pieces in the pan and cook for 2–3 minutes, turning once, until charred. Remove from the pan and keep warm. You will have to do this in batches.

3 Using a small pan, bring the soy sauce, ginger, chilli, sweetener and 3 tablespoons of water to the boil. Add the spring onions and cook for 1–2 minutes until just wilted. Add the aubergines and peppers.

4 Divide the spinach between four plates and top with the aubergine and pepper mixture. Drizzle over any remaining dressing and garnish with the coriander before serving.

Primavera pasta salad

Serves 4
324 calories per serving
Takes 25 minutes

250 g (9 oz) dried pasta
   ribbons
150 g (5½ oz) mange tout
150 g (5½ oz) baby carrots,
   scrubbed
200 g (7 oz) baby corn
150 g (5½ oz) broccoli, cut
   into small florets
4 spring onions, sliced

For the dressing
grated zest and juice of a
   lemon
3 tablespoons virtually fat free
   fromage frais
a small bunch of fresh basil,
   chopped finely
a small bunch of fresh parsley
   or chervil, chopped finely
salt and freshly ground black
   pepper

*A zesty salad, packed full of vital spring vegetables with
gutsy flavours and stimulating textures.*

1 Bring a large saucepan of water to the boil, add the pasta
and cook for 10–15 minutes, or according to the packet
instructions, until al dente.

2 Meanwhile, bring a second large saucepan of water to the
boil, add the mange tout, carrots, baby corn and broccoli and
blanch for 3–5 minutes, until they are just tender. Drain the
pasta and vegetables and place in a large bowl together.

3 Stir all the dressing ingredients together in a small bowl.
Add the dressing to the pasta and vegetable mixture, together
with the spring onions. Toss together, check the seasoning
and then serve warm.

Tip... This salad can be served warm or cold but it is best
warm as the herbs are more aromatic and the vegetables
at their freshest.

Artichoke and chicken salad

Serves 2
184 calories per serving
Takes 30 minutes

1 small red onion, cut into thin
  wedges
calorie controlled cooking
  spray
4 baby courgettes, halved
  lengthways
400 g can artichoke hearts in
  brine, drained and halved
1 tablespoon capers, rinsed
  well
2 tablespoons chopped fresh
  flat leaf parsley
25 g (1 oz) mild piquante
  peppers (e.g. Peppadew),
  drained and sliced finely
100 g (3½ oz) skinless cooked
  chicken breast, sliced thinly
4 tablespoons balsamic
  vinegar
salt and freshly ground black
  pepper

A stunning warm salad for a special lunch or light supper.

1 Put the onion in a bowl and spray with the cooking spray.
Heat a griddle or non stick frying pan until hot and cook the
onion wedges for 3 minutes. Put the courgettes and artichoke
hearts in the bowl and spray with the cooking spray.

2 Turn the onions over and add the courgettes and artichoke
hearts. Cook for a further 5–8 minutes until chargrilled and
tender, turning halfway.

3 Meanwhile, put the capers, parsley and peppers into a bowl.
Add the chargrilled vegetables, toss gently to combine and
season. Divide the chicken slices between two plates and top
each with half the warm chargrilled vegetables.

4 While the griddle or non stick frying pan is still warm, add
the balsamic vinegar to deglaze the pan and bubble for a few
seconds. Drizzle the sticky syrup over the vegetables and
serve.

Ⓥ **Variation...** Replace the cooked chicken with 60 g (2 oz)
of Quorn Deli Chicken Style Slices in step 3.

Index

A

apples:
    celery, tomato and apple soup 22
    parsnip, ham and apple soup 65
artichokes:
    artichoke and chicken salad 170
    tuna and pasta salad with
      artichokes 103
asparagus:
    asparagus and lemon soup 18
    asparagus, Parma ham and
      nectarine salad 162
    watercress and asparagus soup 34
aubergine, spring onion and spinach
    salad 166
avocado and crab salad 124

B

bacon:
    bacon, leek and potato soup 73
    breakfast salad 147
    butter bean and bacon soup 56
    chilli bean salad 118
    hot bacon and plum salad 154
    Manhattan seafood soup 54
    potato salad with bacon 112
    warm broccoli and bacon
      salad 156
beans:
    butter bean and bacon soup 56
    celeriac and butter bean soup 76
    chilli and bean soup 86
    chilli bean salad 118

French broccoli and butter bean
    soup 63
beef:
    main meal minestrone 78
    Sicilian steak salad 139
    Thai beef salad 150
beetroot:
    red hot tomato and beetroot soup
    46
    smoked mackerel and beetroot
      salad 119
Boursin, tomato and turkey salad 92
breakfast salad 147
Brie and courgette soup 82
broccoli:
    French broccoli and butter bean
      soup 63
    primavera pasta salad 168
    warm broccoli and bacon
      salad 156
    warm broccoli and cheese
      salad 153
broths:
    chicken and vegetable broth 66
    hot and sour broth 17
    spicy tortelloni broth 37
    tortelloni and seafood broth 27
bulgar wheat:
    smoked mackerel and beetroot
      salad 119
    tabbouleh salad 104
butter beans:
    butter bean and bacon soup 56

celeriac and butter bean soup 76
French broccoli and butter bean
    soup 63
butternut squash soup 49

C

caesar salad with smoked mackerel
    and Parmesan 101
carrots:
    carrot and spinach soup 32
    creamy carrot and orange soup 40
celeriac and butter bean soup 76
celery, tomato and apple soup 22
cheese:
    Boursin, tomato and turkey
      salad 92
    Brie and courgette soup 82
    caesar salad with smoked
      mackerel and Parmesan 101
    mango, watercress and
      Wensleydale salad 122
    marinated vegetable salad 157
    paprika Feta salad 108–9
    roasted tomato and mozzarella
      salad 132
    warm broccoli and cheese
      salad 153
    warm goat's cheese salad 140
chicken:
    artichoke and chicken salad 170
    chicken and couscous salad 148
    chicken and vegetable broth 66
    chicken and vegetable chowder 52

chicken pasta soup 44
cream of chicken soup 74
hot peppered chicken and
    spinach salad 160
marinated chicken salad 136
Mexican chicken and rice
    salad 111
smoked chicken salad 102
soothing chicken soup 80
tikka chicken salad 116
chick peas:
    Moroccan turkey soup 70
chilled cucumber and mint soup 30
chilli and bean soup 86
chilli bean salad 118
chilli prawn soup 38
chilli vegetable soup 26
chilli, crab and mango salad 94
Chinese prawn and noodle salad 115
chorizo and lentil salad 142
chowders:
    chicken and vegetable chowder 52
    chunky haddock chowder 89
cod:
    spicy fish soup 69
cold soups:
    chilled cucumber and mint soup 30
    gazpacho 20
courgette soup, Brie and 82
couscous:
    chicken and couscous salad 148
    Moroccan turkey soup 70
crab:
    avocado and crab salad 124
    chilli crab and mango salad 94
cream of chicken soup 74

cream of vegetable soup 84
creamy carrot and orange soup 40
cucumber and mint soup, chilled 30

D
duck salad, zingy 159

E
eggs:
    salade Niçoise 120

F
Feta salad, paprika 108–9
fish:
    caesar salad with smoked
        mackerel and Parmesan 101
    chunky haddock chowder 89
    fresh salmon salad 129
    salade Niçoise 120
    smoked mackerel and beetroot
        salad 119
    smoked trout and potato salad 106
    spicy fish soup 69
    tuna and pasta salad with
        artichokes 103
French broccoli and butter bean
    soup 63
fresh salmon salad 129
fruit:
    asparagus and lemon soup 18
    asparagus, Parma ham and
        nectarine salad 162
    celery, tomato and apple soup 22
    chilli, crab and mango salad 94
    creamy carrot and orange soup 40
    hot bacon and plum salad 154

mango, watercress and
    Wensleydale salad 122
parsnip, ham and apple soup 65

G
gazpacho 20
glazed tofu salad 165
glazed turkey salad 143
goat's cheese salad, warm 140
golden onion soup 60

H
haddock chowder, chunky 89
ham:
    asparagus, Parma ham and
        nectarine salad 162
    parsnip, ham and apple soup 65
    pea, mint and ham soup 41
    winter greens soup 43
hot and sour broth 17
hot bacon and plum salad 154
hot peppered chicken and spinach
    salad 160

L
leeks:
    bacon, leek and potato soup 73
    leek and potato soup 62
lemon soup, asparagus and 18
lentils:
    chicken and vegetable chowder
        52
    chorizo and lentil salad 142
    lentil and herb salad 135
    Middle Eastern lentil soup 59
    spicy fish soup 69

M

mackerel:
caesar salad with smoked
mackerel and Parmesan 101
smoked mackerel and beetroot
salad 119
main meal minestrone 78
mango:
chilli, crab and mango salad 94
mango, watercress and
Wensleydale salad 122
Manhattan seafood soup 54
marinated chicken salad 136
marinated vegetable salad 157
Mexican chicken and rice salad 111
Middle Eastern lentil soup 59
minestrone:
main meal minestrone 78
minestrone salad 126
Moroccan turkey soup 70
mozzarella salad, roasted tomato
and 132
mulligatawny soup 77
mushrooms:
breakfast salad 147
mushroom and garlic soup 85

N

nectarine salad, asparagus, Parma
ham and 162
noodles:
chilli prawn soup 38
chilli vegetable soup 26
Chinese prawn and noodle
salad 115
hot and sour broth 17

O

onion soup, golden 60
orange soup, creamy carrot and 40

P

paprika Feta salad 108–9
Parmesan, caesar salad with
smoked mackerel and 101
parsnip, ham and apple soup 65
pasta:
chicken pasta soup 44
main meal minestrone 78
minestrone salad 126
primavera pasta salad 168
roasted pumpkin and pasta salad
144
soupe au pistou 24–5
spicy tortelloni broth 37
tortelloni and seafood broth 27
tuna and pasta salad with
artichokes 103
pea, mint and ham soup 41
plum salad, hot bacon and 154
pork:
breakfast salad 147
chorizo and lentil salad 142
hot and sour broth 17
sweet potato and sausage salad
96
potatoes:
bacon, leek and potato soup 73
leek and potato soup 62
marinated chicken salad 136
marinated vegetable salad 157
potato salad with bacon 112
salade Niçoise 120

smoked trout and potato salad 106
sweet potato and sausage salad 96
prawns:
chilli prawn soup 38
Chinese prawn and noodle
salad 115
tortelloni and seafood broth 27
primavera pasta salad 168
pumpkin and pasta salad,
roasted 144

R

red hot tomato and beetroot soup 46
rice:
Mexican chicken and rice salad
111
soothing chicken soup 80
roasted pumpkin and pasta
salad 144
roasted tomato and mozzarella
salad 132

S

salade Niçoise 120
salads:
artichoke and chicken salad 170
asparagus, Parma ham and
nectarine salad 162
aubergine, spring onion and
spinach salad 166
avocado and crab salad 124
Boursin, tomato and turkey
salad 92
breakfast salad 147
caesar salad with smoked
mackerel and Parmesan 101

chicken and couscous salad 148
chilli bean salad 118
chilli, crab and mango salad 94
Chinese prawn and noodle
    salad 115
chorizo and lentil salad 142
fresh salmon salad 129
glazed tofu salad 165
glazed turkey salad 143
hot bacon and plum salad 154
hot peppered chicken and
    spinach salad 160
lentil and herb salad 135
mango, watercress and
    Wensleydale salad 122
marinated chicken salad 136
marinated vegetable salad 157
Mexican chicken and rice
    salad 111
minestrone salad 126
paprika Feta salad 108–9
potato salad with bacon 112
primavera pasta salad 168
roasted pumpkin and pasta
    salad 144
roasted tomato and mozzarella
    salad 132
salade Niçoise 120
Sicilian steak salad 139
smoked chicken salad 102
smoked mackerel and beetroot
    salad 119
smoked trout and potato salad 106
squid salad 98
sweet potato and sausage salad 96
tabbouleh salad 104

Thai beef salad 150
tikka chicken salad 116
tuna and pasta salad with
    artichokes 103
warm broccoli and bacon
    salad 156
warm broccoli and cheese
    salad 153
warm goat's cheese salad 140
zingy duck salad 159
salmon salad, fresh 129
sausages:
    breakfast salad 147
    sweet potato and sausage salad 96
seafood:
    avocado and crab salad 124
    chilli prawn soup 38
    chilli, crab and mango salad 94
    Chinese prawn and noodle
        salad 115
    Manhattan seafood soup 54
    squid salad 98
    tortelloni and seafood broth 27
Sicilian steak salad 139
smoked chicken salad 102
smoked mackerel and beetroot
    salad 119
smoked trout and potato salad 106
soothing chicken soup 80
soupe au pistou 24–5
soups:
    asparagus and lemon soup 18
    bacon, leek and potato soup 73
    Brie and courgette soup 82
    butter bean and bacon soup 56
    butternut squash soup 49

carrot and spinach soup 32
celeriac and butter bean soup 76
celery, tomato and apple soup 22
chicken and vegetable broth 66
chicken and vegetable
    chowder 52
chicken pasta soup 44
chilled cucumber and mint soup 30
chilli and bean soup 86
chilli prawn soup 38
chilli vegetable soup 26
chunky haddock chowder 89
cream of chicken soup 74
cream of vegetable soup 84
creamy carrot and orange soup 40
French broccoli and butter bean
    soup 63
gazpacho 20
golden onion soup 60
hot and sour broth 17
leek and potato soup 62
main meal minestrone 78
Manhattan seafood soup 54
Middle Eastern lentil soup 59
Moroccan turkey soup 70
mulligatawny soup 77
mushroom and garlic soup 85
parsnip, ham and apple soup 65
pea, mint and ham soup 41
red hot tomato and beetroot
    soup 46
soothing chicken soup 80
soupe au pistou 24–5
spicy fish soup 69
spicy tortelloni broth 37
sweet tomato and basil soup 29

Thai spinach soup 14
tortelloni and seafood broth 27
watercress and asparagus soup 34
winter greens soup 43
spicy fish soup 69
spicy tortelloni broth 37
spinach:
aubergine, spring onion and
spinach salad 166
carrot and spinach soup 32
hot peppered chicken and
spinach salad 160
Thai spinach soup 14
spring onion and spinach salad,
aubergine 166
squash soup, butternut 49
squid salad 98
steak salad, Sicilian 139
sweet potatoes:
marinated chicken salad 136
marinated vegetable salad 157
sweet potato and sausage
salad 96
sweet tomato and basil soup 29

T
tabbouleh salad 104
Thai beef salad 150

Thai spinach soup 14
tikka chicken salad 116
tofu:
chilli vegetable soup 26
glazed tofu salad 165
tomatoes:
Boursin, tomato and turkey
salad 92
breakfast salad 147
celery, tomato and apple soup 22
gazpacho 20
red hot tomato and beetroot
soup 46
roasted tomato and mozzarella
salad 132
sweet tomato and basil soup 29
tortelloni and seafood broth 27
trout and potato salad, smoked
106
tuna:
salade Niçoise 120
tuna and pasta salad with
artichokes 103
turkey:
Boursin, tomato and turkey
salad 92
glazed turkey salad 143
Moroccan turkey soup 70

V
vegetables:
chicken and vegetable broth 66
chicken and vegetable
chowder 52
chilli vegetable soup 26
cream of vegetable soup 84
marinated vegetable salad 157
minestrone salad 126
primavera pasta salad 168
winter greens soup 43

W
warm broccoli and bacon salad 156
warm broccoli and cheese salad
153
warm goat's cheese salad 140
watercress:
mango, watercress and
Wensleydale salad 122
watercress and asparagus
soup 34
Wensleydale salad, mango,
watercress and 122
winter greens soup 43

Z
zingy duck salad 159